Vintage Baby Knits

MORE THAN 40 HEIRLOOM PATTERNS FROM THE 1920s TO THE 1950s

Kristen Rengren

PHOTOGRAPHY BY
THAYER ALLYSON GOWDY

WARDROBE STYLING AND SET DESIGN BY
VIKTORIA RUCHKAN

STC CRAFT/A MELANIE FALICK BOOK
STEWART, TABORI & CHANG
NEW YORK

Published in 2009 by Stewart, Tabori & Chang
An imprint of Harry N. Abrams, Inc.

Text and illustrations copyright © 2009 by Kristen Rengren
Photographs copyright © 2009 by Thayer Allyson Gowdy

Library of Congress Cataloging-in-Publication Data

Rengren, Kristen.
Vintage Baby Knits / Kristen Rengren ; photography by Thayer Allyson Gowdy.
p. cm.
ISBN 978-1-58479-761-6 (alk. paper)
1. Knitting--Patterns. 2. Infants' clothing. I. Title.

TT825.R424 2009
746.43'2041--dc22
2008028231

Editor: Melanie Falick
Designer: Onethread
Production Manager: Jacqueline Poirier

The text of this book was composed in Futura, Caslon, and Amazon.

Printed and bound in China
10 9 8 7 6 5 4 3 2 1

HNA
harry n. abrams, inc.
a subsidiary of La Martinière Groupe

115 West 18th Street, New York, NY 10011
www.hnabooks.com

INTRODUCTION
4

CHAPTER ONE
GETTING READY TO KNIT
6

CHAPTER TWO
PROJECTS TO KNIT FOR BABY
11

CHAPTER THREE
RESOURCES
149

ABBREVIATIONS
157

SPECIAL TECHNIQUES
158

ACKNOWLEDGMENTS
159

ABOUT THE AUTHOR
160

Introduction

The first time I saw a vintage knitting pattern booklet, I was captivated. "Are you sure you want all of those?" asked the lady whose garage-sale collection I was cleaning out, as I handed over every last laundry quarter in my pocket. I didn't need clean laundry. I was in love.

I've admired vintage clothing for as long as I can remember, and by the summer when I spotted those first pattern booklets, I'd already been knitting for ten years—but my two passions had never really connected before. And, all of a sudden, I had a wonderful idea—I would make "vintage" clothes from scratch by updating old patterns!

From that moment forward, I hunted high and low for this new quarry. I was already working as a vintage clothing dealer, which meant I spent much of my time milling about estate sales before dawn, combing through thrift stores, and scouring eBay at all hours to find trim Dior suits, slinky Schiaparelli gowns, and other vintage treasures to send off to boutiques in New York and Hollywood. By multitasking and searching out pattern booklets at the same time, within two years I was able to collect hundreds of them from the 1920s through the 1950s.

The baby pattern booklets—loaded with black-and-white photos of babies in handknits, as well as lively illustrations of frolicking tots, friendly zoo animals, and smiling storks—always intrigued me most. The projects were classic and simple in style, yet detailed enough to hold even a highly distractible knitter's interest, and I could easily imagine modern babies wearing them.

I spent months studying those patterns. Most called for a long-forgotten yarn, such as 5 ounces of Lady Betty or Germantown Zephyr, and a particular needle size, but did not specify fiber content, yardage, or gauge, or even include a schematic. I read each pattern word by word, sketching my own schematics along the way, in order to understand the project's construction. I created charts where there were none. And I compared one pattern to another in order to learn about the styles and knitting conventions of the day. Then I began swatching with modern yarns of different gauges and fibers to determine which would work best for each project.

I went through this process for more projects than could ever fit into this book in order to determine which ones would work together to make the best collection. Once I had narrowed down my options, I began testing each pattern, correcting, revising, and resizing as necessary to suit the modern knitter (and baby), all the while striving to maintain the classic spirit of the original design. Wherever possible, I addressed issues of safety (removing buttons and ties) and convenience (for instance, making sure that garments would be easy to get on and off). Some patterns required only moderate adaptations, such as figuring out the gauge, choosing a yarn, and adding multiple sizes (since many of these patterns were originally written for only one or two sizes), while others required overhauls that were more extensive in order to be usable today. From time to time, a pattern didn't work at all and had to be rewritten completely.

While I did include some quick-to-knit projects, the majority of the patterns from this period seem to have been knitted at much finer gauges than a knitter today might be accustomed to. A few patterns called for "Jiffy-Knit" or bulky yarns, but most called for the equivalent of today's fingering-weight yarn. Accordingly, many of the projects in this book are knitted to gauges that may seem small to the modern knitter. But because baby garments are so small, even at finer gauges they can be worked quickly—and the results are not only handsome and durable, but also boast true vintage style.

While my collection of vintage pattern booklets is large, vintage patterns are actually rarer than you might imagine. Yarn companies in the 1920s through 1950s published pattern booklets by the thousands each month, but the average knitter discarded them at season's end. When I visited the U.S. Copyright Office at the Library of Congress to painstakingly check the copyright status of each book I had acquired, I was stunned to learn that rarely if ever had their copyrights been renewed—if the original copyright had been applied for at all. The companies that published these wonderful patterns did not seem to see the value in preserving them. Moreover, with very few exceptions, the booklets did not credit the projects' designers. Their endless creativity went unrecognized, except by the millions of women who gratefully knit their designs.

It is to these talented individuals that I dedicate *Vintage Baby Knits*. I can only hope that they would be pleased by my efforts to recreate their work and to share it here. I hope that you will enjoy these patterns as much as I have, and that the projects you knit from them will become cherished treasures for generations to come.

CHAPTER ONE

Getting Ready to Knit

Here are some pointers to consider before
casting on. Follow them and you'll be sure to knit something
that will be cherished for many years to come.

CHOOSING THE RIGHT PATTERN FOR BABY—AND FOR YOU

There's something in *Vintage Baby Knits* to meet every knitter's mood and every baby's style and needs. You will find unusual patterns that include cables, lace, colorwork, textured stitches, and more, as well as some wonderfully simple patterns too. When choosing a pattern from this book, you'll notice that there are no levels of difficulty listed—because if you can knit and purl, you can learn to make every pattern here. That's one of the beauties of baby patterns—you can experiment with techniques you've never tried before, and because baby things are so tiny, you don't have to invest a lot of time or money. They're so small that you'll be done before you know it!

BUT WHAT SIZE SHOULD I MAKE?

Before you get started, there are a few factors to consider regarding size. People grow big babies nowadays. Although the 0 to 3 month size is useful for very small babies and for garments that absolutely need to be worn just after birth, like a christening gown, many babies simply never fit into it. If the baby hasn't yet been born, or if you have an inkling that he or she is going to be a big one, consider making a 3 to 6 month or even a 6 to 12 month size. Another consideration is the age the baby will be when the garment will be worn. If you are knitting a winter sweater for a June baby, make sure you choose a size large enough to fit the baby when the time comes. Next, think about your own knitting ability and a realistic time frame for finishing the project. Finally, when in doubt, knit big. Babies grow amazingly quickly, and you want to have a garment that will last for a good long while. They can always grow into a garment that is large at first. For a chart of average baby sizes today, see page 153.

CHOOSING YARN

Next to sizing, yarn is the most important decision you will make when creating your project. I took great care to choose yarns that look and feel good for the projects in this book. Should you want or need to substitute, consider this sage advice.

First, knit with the best yarn you can afford. The "best" doesn't necessarily mean the most expensive—it means yarn that looks and feels nice and will wear well. Generally, I prefer natural fibers and blends of natural fibers with high-quality synthetics. In my opinion, cheap acrylics—long considered the standard for baby wear—present some real problems. Most importantly,

they sometimes don't wear well, losing their shape and pilling. A beautiful pattern in cheap yarn is going to look and feel like a cheap thing. I'm also not usually a big fan of baby projects made out of super expensive luxury yarn. The temptation is understandable—babies are special, and one way we can show how we feel is by sparing no expense and choosing the most luxurious fiber around. That's fine as long as we're comfortable with the idea that what we make will probably need to be hand-washed. On the rare occasion that I do choose a luxury yarn, I stick with yarns with multiple plies (strands that are twisted together), rather than unplied and single-ply yarns, which tend to pill easily.

Wool

There are people who believe wool is too coarse for baby, but that's a misconception. Go to any well-stocked yarn shop and start touching the wool, and you will be sure to find some very soft choices. In fact, the softest Merino baby yarn can feel about as soft as most cashmere. Wool is also lightweight (much lighter than cotton, in fact), so it is an excellent choice for layering. The separate fibers of wool cross one another and trap pockets of air, helping to regulate body temperature, so that it feels cool in summer and warm in winter—making it wearable by baby in three or even four seasons. Wool also absorbs and wicks away moisture, and dries quickly. That's why, in the days before disposable diapers, diaper covers—known as soaker pants—were made out of wool and not cotton.

In the past, some people would choose acrylic over wool because only acrylic could be machine-washed, but these days it's easy to find washable wools. In addition, the no-rinse wool washes now on the market make hand-washing much less laborious than it used to be.

My personal favorite yarn for baby knits is wool sock yarn. Made from especially soft and fine wool, sometimes reinforced with nylon for durability, and produced in myriad colors, sock yarn knits up at a gauge similar to that of vintage patterns for many baby items. It usually wears like a dream, and is also usually machine-washable.

Some folks think that letting a baby near wool risks giving baby an allergy to it later in life, but wool allergies among babies are actually pretty rare. Sensitivities to rough wool, however, are much more common. So unless you know that Mom or Dad already has an allergy, or you have some other reason to suspect an allergy might be in the works, don't fear giving baby woolly things—just make them out of the softest wool you can find. To test wool, hold the ball up against your cheek to see if it feels soft enough for a baby.

Cotton and Cotton Blends

In the eighteenth and nineteenth centuries, many children's sweaters were knitted out of cotton yarns. Yet by the mid-twentieth century, cotton was only rarely knitted into garments. Cotton was instead reserved for home items such as tablecloths and dish towels, and was only occasionally used to make accessories such as slippers. Part of the reason lies in cotton's relative lack of stretch. Getting an unyielding cotton garment on a wriggling baby could be quite difficult. Cotton also fell out of favor because it feels cold when wet—and babies are often wet! Today's cotton can make an excellent substitute for wool yarn as long as these caveats are considered: When substituting cotton for wool, remember that pure cotton doesn't stretch much. Use it only where you can get baby in and out of it easily, and use patterns that have some natural elasticity, like ribbing. Another alternative is to use a yarn made of cotton blended with wool, or cotton blended with a synthetic fiber like Lycra or spandex that will lend it some stretch. Also remember that pure cotton is much heavier than wool, which may weigh a garment down and distort the shape of bulkier items, such as some cabled sweaters.

Two synthetic fibers derived from natural materials make excellent additions to cotton in blends. Lyocell (known commercially as Tencel) and Modal are both made from cellulose. They both make cotton stronger, lighter, and softer, while lending wonderful drape and sheen. They do not add much stretch, however, so if you need stretch, look for a blend that includes a little Lycra or spandex.

Linen and Hemp

In my opinion, linen, which is a plant fiber, is one of the best baby yarns you'll ever encounter. It's machine-washable and -dryable—excellent qualities for any baby garment. Linen is hypoallergenic, so it's a great choice when you think there might be an allergy issue. Unlike cotton, it is lightweight. And, in addition to draping beautifully, it's incredibly soft when washed—and it gets softer with each use. Admittedly, it sometimes feels quite stiff in the skein, but once you wash it, it can be softer than a baby's bottom. Linen doesn't stretch the way wool does, so substitute linen where you would use another nonstretchy fiber like cotton.

Hemp may not have been widely used when the patterns in this book were originally written, but it is another fine choice for babies. Like linen, it feels stiff in the skein but becomes incredibly soft upon repeated washing and drying, and it is nearly indestructible. It's cool in the summer and warm in the winter. It also keeps its shape no matter what—no shrinking and no stretching. Best of all, almost all hemp for knitting yarn is grown organically. Consider hemp as a substitute in any pattern calling for linen or cotton. Like linen, it won't have the stretch that wool does, and it is much heavier, so it should not be used as a substitute for wool.

Manufactured Fibers from Natural Materials

There are several other natural fibers that make excellent yarns for baby. Three thoroughly modern yarns stand out: Bamboo is wonderfully soft and durable and drapes beautifully. Despite the fact that most manufacturers specify that it needs to be hand-washed on their ball bands, I find that it usually machine-washes and -dries quite nicely. Corn is another fiber that works well for babies. It's unbelievably soft and light, keeps its shape well, and is machine-washable and dryable. Soy silk is a soft, strong, and light yarn with similar durability and drape to wool. And all three are vegan and environmentally sustainable.

Tools

"Knitting is an art that requires but a few, inexpensive tools," wrote the legendary knitwear designer Alice Carroll in her 1947 book *The Complete Guide to Modern Knitting and Crocheting*. "It is wise, then, that these few be of the best type and quality." Today as yesterday, the right tools can make or break a knitter. Here are the ones you'll need to complete the projects in this book.

Knitting Needles

While the aluminum needles of yesteryear are cool to look at and perfectly serviceable for flat knitting, there are many new needle choices available to the knitter. My personal favorites are stainless-steel or nickel-plated circular needles. They are versatile enough to be used either to knit flat or in the round, and they are easier on my hands than straight needles. I love hardwood double-pointed needles for their warmth and flexibility, but because I have a tight grip that can be dangerous for thin wooden needles, I tend to use steel needles in smaller sizes instead. Ultimately, each knitter needs to choose what suits him or her best. You may prefer the grabbiness of bamboo, the smooth matte surface of hardwood, or the slipperiness of nickel or steel.

Crochet Hook

When you slip up, a crochet hook can be your best friend. Use it to pick up dropped stitches or untwist a twisted stitch, as well as to cast on stitches for a neat and attractive selvedge edge.

Tapestry Needle

Use this handy little tool (which looks like a giant sewing needle) to weave in ends when you're done knitting, to sew your projects together, and to graft live stitches together.

Measuring Tape

Measuring tapes are tools you won't want to buy vintage. They stretch out with age—so treat yourself to a fresh one every couple of years.

Needle Gauge

Because needles come in so many sizes, and because many needles lose their markings over time, it's important to have a needle gauge. Some needle gauges can also be used to measure stitch and row gauge and/or other small areas. Look for a gauge that gives measurements in metric as well as in US needle sizes.

Cable Needle

This curved or U-shaped needle is a handy tool for holding stitches while cabling—but in a pinch, you can do what vintage patterns suggest and use an extra double-pointed needle instead.

Scissors

Get a good pair of embroidery scissors to cut your yarn with, and keep them sharp by never, ever using them to cut anything that isn't yarn.

Stitch Holders

Back in the day, people used scraps of waste yarn to serve as stitch holders—but you'll likely find the modern stitch holder (which looks like a giant safety pin) easier to handle.

Stitch Markers

These handy little devices slip onto knitting needles or directly onto the knitted fabric to help you keep track of what you are doing while you're working. Whether you choose fancy handmade markers or plain plastic ones, no knitting bag is complete without them. Although in the past knitters would have simply used a contrasting piece of yarn, today you can choose among plain rings, split-ring, and locking stitch markers. I prefer the locking stitch markers because they can also be used to hold a live stitch or two in a pinch, and because they are handy to mark the right side of a garment or to hold together pieces to be seamed.

A lot of people don't like swatching, but it's crucial to your success when knitting baby items. First, even if you are using the suggested yarn for a pattern, a swatch is critical to discovering whether or not you have the right gauge. Every knitter is different, and what's more, every yarn is different—meaning that even if you got spot-on gauge for your last three projects, unless you're using the exact same yarn, needles, and stitch pattern, you might not get it for this one. And with baby garments, gauge is even more critical than with adult garments because they are so small. Let's say you are shooting for a gauge of 8 stitches to the inch (2.5 cm), but you're really getting 7 stitches to the inch (2.5 cm) instead. If you go ahead and knit a baby sweater that calls for 160 stitches at the chest, you won't get a 20" (51 cm) garment as planned for—you'll get a sweater that's 23" (58.5 cm) around. That's the difference between a size for a six-month-old baby and a two-year-old toddler!

Furthermore, yarn isn't cheap. What if you hate the yarn you're working with? What if you've made a substitution, but the texture or drape or weight is all wrong? There are two ways and two ways only to know these things: You can knit a swatch, and find out if it works for you, or you can knit the whole garment and risk suffering intense disappointment if your hours of knitting turn into a waste of time because the garment turns out all wrong. So avoid unnecessary heartbreak and knit a swatch before you start. You can always buy just one ball of yarn to test it out before you commit to a large purchase and a lot of time.

To make a swatch, cast on enough stitches to make at least a 5-6" (12.5-15 cm) piece of fabric, and knit for a minimum of 5" (12.5 cm) before you bind off again. When you're done—and here is another step you simply cannot skip—wash and dry your swatch as the finished project is meant to be washed and dried. It's important to know what the yarn will look like once you've taken care of it the way you will the garment—otherwise it might look great on the first wear and not so great thereafter.

CHAPTER TWO

Projects to Knit for Baby

Pearl Shrug
12

Billie Beret
16

Floyd Pullover
18

Audrey Hoodie
22

Milo Soakers
26

Stella Pixie Hat
30

Rufus Textured Cardigan
32

Louise Cardigan
36

Liza Sideways Sacque
40

Jasper Diamond Hoodie
44

Betty Lou Lace Cardigan
48

Violet Sacque
52

Rupert the Lion &
Elmer the Elephant
56

Bunny Blanket
62

Horace the Horse
66

Dewey Cabled Pullover
70

Cleo Kitty Slippers
74

Felix Cardigan & Pants Set
76

Maude Honeycomb Blanket
82

Daisy Soakers
86

Otto Short-Sleeved
Pullover & Archie Vest
90

Hazel Cape
96

Bobby Kimono
100

Harry Sailor Sweater
104

Monty Snowsuit
with Cap & Mittens
108

Ducky Onesie
114

Frankie Striped Socks
118

Jackie Cabled Set
122

Gladys Fair Isle Bonnet
128

Twyla Shoulderette
132

Oscar Argyle Sweater
136

Avery Christening
Gown & Frock
140

Frances Nursing Shawl
146

Pearl Shrug

THE CLEVER CONSTRUCTION OF THIS DARLING SHRUG MAKES IT FUN TO KNIT.
IT IS STARTED IN AN HOURGLASS SHAPE AT THE CENTER BACK, THEN SLEEVES ARE WORKED IN A CONICAL PATTERN
IN THE ROUND. IT ONLY COMES TOGETHER WHEN YOU WORK THE LACY DROP-STITCH BORDER
AROUND THE EDGE. THE ORIGINAL 1950S PATTERN ALSO INCLUDED AN IDENTICAL MATCHING SHRUG SIZED FOR MOM,
MEANT TO BE WORN AS A BED JACKET IN THE DAYS AND WEEKS OF RECOVERY FROM GIVING BIRTH.

SIZES
3-6 months (6-12 months)
Shown in size 3-6 months

FINISHED MEASUREMENTS
To fit 18 (19)" [45 (48) cm] chest

YARN
Lorna's Laces Shepherd Sock (80% super-wash wool / 20% nylon; 215 yards [196 meters] / 2 ounces [57 grams]): 2 hanks #53NS Whisper

NEEDLES
3–6 MONTHS:
One pair straight needles size US 2 (2.75 mm)
One 24" (60 cm) long circular (circ) needle size US 2 (2.75 mm)
Change needle size if necessary to obtain correct gauge.

9–12 MONTHS:
One pair straight needles size US 3 (3.25 mm)
One 24" (60 cm) long circular (circ) needle size US 3 (3.25 mm)
Change needle size if necessary to obtain correct gauge.

NOTIONS
Crochet hook size C-2 (D-3) [2.75 (3.25) mm); stitch marker

GAUGE
3–6 MONTHS:
32 sts and 49 rows = 4" (10 cm) in Broken Rib, using smaller needles

9–12 MONTHS:
30 sts and 46 rows = 4" (10 cm) in Broken Rib, using larger needles

NOTE
Instructions are the same for both sizes; use the smaller needles for the 3-6 month size and the larger needles for the 9-12 month size.

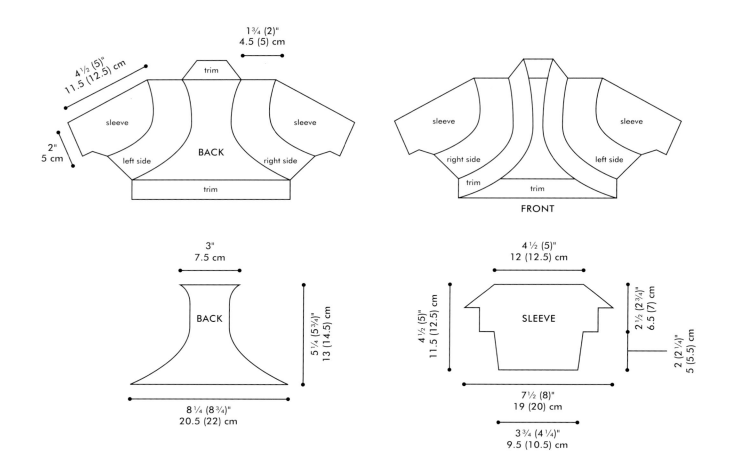

STITCH PATTERNS

Broken Rib (multiple of 2 sts + 1; 2-row repeat)
Row 1 (RS): K1, *p1, k1; repeat from * to end.
Row 2: Purl.
Repeat Rows 1 and 2 for Broken Rib.

Garter Openwork Pattern (multiple of 2 sts + 1; 4-row repeat)
Row 1 (RS): K1, *yo, wrapping yarn around needle 4 times, k1; repeat from * to end.
Row 2: Knit, dropping all yo's.
Rows 3 and 4: Knit.
Repeat Rows 1-4 for Garter Openwork Pattern.

BACK

Using straight needles, CO 65 sts. Begin Broken Rib. Work even for 2 rows.
Shape Back (RS): BO 2 sts at beginning of next 14 rows, then decrease 1 st each side every other row 11 times–15 sts remain. Work even for 14 rows.
Next Row (RS): Increase 1 st each side this row, every other row once, then every 4 rows twice, ending with a WS row–23 sts.
BO 22 sts–1 st remains. Do not break yarn.

LEFT SIDE

With RS facing, 1 st on right-hand needle, and using circ needle, beginning at BO edge of Back, pick up and knit 63 sts along left side of Back, using Cable CO (see Special Techniques, page 158), CO 72 sts–136 sts. Join for working in the rnd, being careful not to twist sts; place marker (pm) for beginning of rnd.
Rnd 1: *K1, p1; repeat from * to end.
Rnd 2: Knit.
Rnds 3-10: Repeat Rnds 1 and 2.
Rnd 11: Repeat Rnd 1.
Rnd 12: *K2, k2tog; repeat from * to end–102 sts remain.

Rnds 13-20: Repeat Rnds 1 and 2.

Rnd 21: Repeat Rnd 1.

Rnd 22: BO all sts loosely as follows: K2tog, *k2tog, pass first st over second st; repeat from * to end. Fasten off.

RIGHT SIDE

With RS facing, using a circ needle beginning at CO edge of Back, pick up and knit 64 sts along right side of Back, CO 72 sts—136 sts. Complete as for Left Side.

NECK/BODY TRIM

Divide remaining yarn into 2 equal balls. With RS facing, using circ needle and 2 strands of yarn held together, pick up and knit 32 sts along lower edge of Back, 36 sts along Right Side, 21 sts along upper edge of Back, and 36 sts along Left Side—125 sts. Join for working in the rnd; pm for beginning of rnd. *Note: You may use multiple double-pointed needles instead of circ needle.*

Rnds 1, 3, 7, and 9: Knit.

Rnds 2 and 4: Purl.

Rnd 5: *K1, yo, wrapping yarn 4 times around needle; repeat from * to end of rnd.

Rnd 6: Purl, dropping all yo's.

Rnd 8: *P5, p1-f/b; repeat from * to last 5 sts, p5—145 sts.

Rnd 10: Purl. BO all sts as follows: With crochet hook, ch1 into first st on needle, slipping st from needle, *sc into next 2 sts, ch1; repeat from * to last 2 sts, sc into next 2 sts. Fasten off last st.

SLEEVES

Using straight needles and 2 strands of yarn held together, CO 21 sts. Knit 1 row.

Next Row (WS): *K4, k1-f/b; repeat from * to last st, k1—25 sts.

Next Row: Begin Garter Openwork Pattern. Work even for 1 row.

Shape Sleeve (WS): Continuing in Garter Openwork Pattern, CO 4 sts at beginning of next

2 rows, working CO sts into pattern—33 sts. Work even for 1 row.

(RS) Repeat last 4 rows once—41 sts. Repeat Rows 1 and 2 of Garter Openwork Pattern once.

Next Row (RS): *K2, k2tog; repeat from * to last st, k1—31 sts remain. Work Row 4, then Rows 1 and 2 of Garter Openwork Pattern.

Next Row (RS): *K4, k2tog; repeat from * to last st, k1—26 sts remain.

Next Row (WS): Change to Garter st (knit every row). Work even for 3 rows. BO all sts loosely.

FINISHING

Sew in Sleeves. Sew Sleeve seams. Block lightly.

Billie Beret

WARM HATS ARE A MUST FOR THE WINTER BABY. THIS 1936 DESIGN
FROM THE COLUMBIA YARN COMPANY FEATURES A SIMPLE
KNIT-PURL TEXTURE. IT IS TYPICAL OF THE TAMS AND BERETS THAT WERE
DE RIGUEUR FOR CHILDREN IN THE 1930S. HERE IT IS WORKED IN SOFT WASHABLE
WOOL AT A CLOSER GAUGE THAN GENERALLY USED FOR THIS YARN,
IN ORDER TO CREATE A WARM AND COZY FABRIC THAT IS SURE TO KEEP BABY'S HEAD TOASTY.

SIZES
6-12 months
(12-18 months, 18-24 months)
Shown in size 12-18 months

FINISHED MEASUREMENTS
14 ½ (15 ¾, 17 ¼)" [37 (40, 44) cm]
circumference

YARN
Dale of Norway Baby Ull
(100% superwash Merino wool; 192 yards
[175 meters] / 50 grams): 1 (2, 2) skeins
#6714 Bright Turquoise

NEEDLES
One set of five doubled-pointed needles
(dpn) size US 0 (2 mm)
One set of five doubled-pointed needles
size US 1 (2.25 mm)
One 16" (40 cm) circular (circ) needle size
US 1 (2.25 mm)
One 24" (60 cm) circular needle size
US 1 (2.25 mm)
Change needle size if necessary to obtain
correct gauge.

NOTIONS
Stitch marker

GAUGE
36 sts and 56 rows = 4" (10 cm) in Ridge
Pattern, using larger needles

STITCH PATTERNS
Ridge Pattern (multiple of 8 sts; 8-rnd repeat)
Rnds 1 and 2: *K2, p6; repeat from * to end.
Rnds 3 and 4: Knit.
Rnds 5 and 6: *P4, k2, p2; repeat from * to end.
Rnds 7 and 8: Knit.
Repeat Rnds 1-8 for Ridge Pattern.

1x1 Rib (multiple of 2 sts; 1-rnd repeat)
All Rnds: *K1, p1; repeat from * to end.

2x2 Rib (multiple of 4 sts; 1-rnd repeat)
All Rnds: *K2, p2; repeat from * to end.

BERET

Using smaller dpns, CO 174 (190, 206) sts. Join for working in the rnd, being careful not to twist sts; place marker (pm) for beginning of rnd. Begin 1x1 Rib. Work even until piece measures ¾" (2 cm) from the beginning.

Note: Change to circular needle, then to dpns, when appropriate for number of sts on needle.

Increase Rnd: Change to larger needles. *K17 (19, 20), M1; repeat from * to last 4 (0, 6) sts, knit to end−184 (200, 216) sts.

Next Rnd: Change to Ridge Pattern. Work even until piece measures 2¾ (3, 3¼)" [7 (7.5, 8.5) cm] from the beginning.

Next Rnd: Change to smaller needles. Work even for ½" (1 cm).

Next Rnd: Change to 1x1 Rib. Work even for ½" (1 cm).

Decrease Rnd 1: *K2tog, p2tog; repeat from * to end−92 (100, 108) sts remain.

Next Rnd: Change to 2x2 Rib. Work even for ½" (1 cm).

Next Rnd: Repeat Decrease Rnd 1−46 (50, 54) sts remain.

Next Rnd: Change to 2x2 Rib; work to last 2 sts, k1, p1. Work even for ½" (2 cm).

Decrease Rnd 2: *K2tog, p2tog; repeat from * to last 2 sts, k1, p1−24 (26, 28) sts remain.

Next Rnd: Change to 2x2 Rib, decrease 0 (2, 0) sts at end of first rnd−24 (24, 28) sts remain. Break yarn, leaving a long tail. Thread tail through remaining sts twice, pull tight and fasten off, with tail to WS.

Floyd Pullover

THE SIMPLEST OF ALL SWEATERS, THE BODY OF THIS 1931 DROP-SHOULDER
PULLOVER IS WORKED IN ONE PIECE, THEN SEAMED UP THE SIDES, WITH STITCHES PICKED UP
FOR SLEEVES. USING NOTHING BUT SIMPLE GARTER STITCH AND STOCKINETTE STITCH,
THE PATTERN FORMS A SUBTLE, ATTRACTIVE DIAMOND MOTIF AT THE
TOP AND BOTTOM OF THE BODY.

SIZES
3-6 months
(6-12 months, 12-18 months)
Shown in size 12-18 months

FINISHED MEASUREMENTS
19 (21, 23 ½)"
[48.5 (53.5, 59.5) cm] chest

YARN
Artyarns Supermerino (100% Merino wool;
104 yards [95 meters] / 50 grams):
2 (3, 3) hanks #263

NEEDLES
One pair straight needles size US 5
(3.75 mm)
One pair straight needles size US 6 (4 mm)
Change needle size if necessary
to obtain correct gauge.

NOTIONS
Removable stitch markers

GAUGE
22 sts and 44 rows = 4" (10 cm) in Garter
stitch (knit every row), using larger needles
23 sts and 28 rows = 4" (10 cm) in
Stockinette stitch (St st), using larger needles

BACK AND FRONT (both alike)
Using larger needles, CO 55 (61, 67) sts.
Begin Garter st (knit every row). Work even
for 18 rows.
Begin Diamond Pattern (WS): Work across
Diamond Chart, beginning with st# 3 (11, 4)
of Chart, reading from left to right, and ending
with st# 9 (1, 8). Work even until Rows 1-9 of
Chart are complete.
Next Row (RS): Change to St st. Work even
until piece measures 8½ (9, 9½)" [21.5 (23, 24.5)
cm] from the beginning, ending with a RS row.
Begin Diamond Pattern (WS): Change to
smaller needles. Work across Diamond Chart,
beginning with Row 9, st# 3 (11, 4) of Chart, and
ending with st# 9 (1, 8). Work even until Rows
9-17 of Chart are complete.

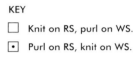

KEY

☐ Knit on RS, purl on WS.

⊡ Purl on RS, knit on WS.

DIAMOND CHART

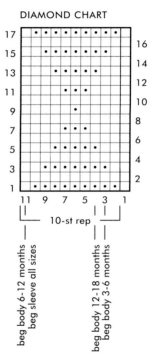

10-st rep

beg body 6-12 months
beg sleeve all sizes

beg body 12-18 months
beg body 3-6 months

Next Row (RS): Change to Garter st. Work even until piece measures 12 (12¾, 13½)" [30.5 (32.5, 34.5) cm] from the beginning, ending with a WS row.

Shape Neck (RS): Work 13 (15, 17) sts, join a second ball of yarn, BO center 29 (31, 33) sts, work to end. Working both sides at the same time, work even until piece measures 13 (13¾, 14½)" [33 (35, 37) cm] from the beginning, ending with a WS row. BO all sts.

SLEEVES

Sew shoulder seams. Place marker 4½ (4¾, 5)" [11.5 (12, 12.5) cm] down from shoulder seams on Front and Back (at base of Garter st diamond on yoke). Using larger needles, pick up and knit 53 (55, 57) sts between markers. Begin St st, beginning with a purl row. Work even for 1" (2.5 cm), ending with a WS row.

Shape Sleeves (RS): Decrease 1 st each side this row, then every 12 (12, 10) rows 5 (6, 7) times, as follows: K1, ssk, work to last 3 sts, k2tog, k1—41 sts remain. Work even until piece measures 6¼ (6¾, 7¼)" [16 (17, 18.5) cm] from pick-up row, ending with a RS row.

Next Row (WS): Change to smaller needles and Garter st. Work even for 6 rows.

Begin Diamond Pattern (WS): Work across Diamond Chart. Work even until entire Chart is complete.

Next Row (RS): Change to Garter st. Work even for 6 rows. BO all sts.

FINISHING

Block piece to measurements. Sew side and Sleeve seams.

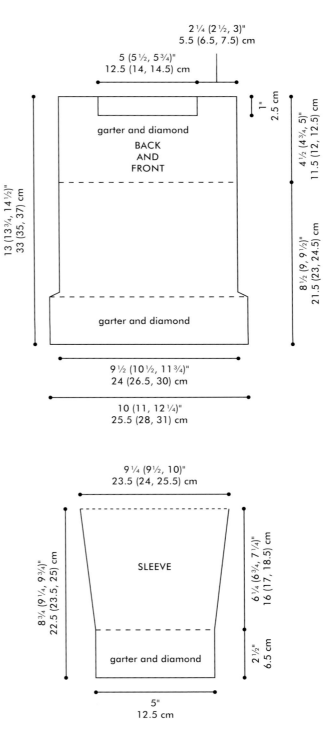

2¼ (2½, 3)"
5.5 (6.5, 7.5) cm

5 (5½, 5¾)"
12.5 (14, 14.5) cm

1"
2.5 cm

4½ (4¾, 5)"
11.5 (12, 12.5) cm

garter and diamond
BACK
AND
FRONT

13 (13¾, 14½)"
33 (35, 37) cm

8½ (9, 9½)"
21.5 (23, 24.5) cm

garter and diamond

9½ (10½, 11¾)"
24 (26.5, 30) cm

10 (11, 12¼)"
25.5 (28, 31) cm

9¼ (9½, 10)"
23.5 (24, 25.5) cm

SLEEVE

8¾ (9¼, 9¾)"
22.5 (23.5, 25) cm

6¼ (6¾, 7¼)"
16 (17, 18.5) cm

garter and diamond

2½"
6.5 cm

5"
12.5 cm

Audrey Hoodie

THIS SIMPLE SEED-STITCH HOODIE FROM 1957 IS AN EXAMPLE OF THE QUICK-TO-KNIT
PATTERNS SO POPULAR IN THE LATE 1950S. WITH TELEVISION AND OTHER CONCERNS OF MODERN LIFE CAME
LESS PATIENCE FOR KNITTING, AND PATTERNS LIKE THESE CATERED TO THE KNITTER WITH A SHORT
ATTENTION SPAN. IF YOU'VE NEVER WORKED A SHELL EDGING IN CROCHET BEFORE, PRACTICE ON YOUR
SWATCH UNTIL YOU FEEL COMFORTABLE WITH IT. THE SWEATER IS MEANT TO BE WORN OPEN,
WITH CUFFS THAT ROLL BACK SO BABY HAS ROOM TO GROW.

SIZES
3-6 months (6-9 months)
Shown in size 3-6 months

FINISHED MEASUREMENTS
18 (19 ½)" [45.5 (49.5) cm] chest

YARN
Cascade Yarns Arcadia DK (80% Pima
cotton / 20% angora; 116 yards
[106 meters] / 50 grams): 3 skeins #4201

NEEDLES
One pair straight needles
size US 5 (3.75 cm)
Change needle size if necessary
to obtain correct gauge.

NOTIONS
Crochet hook size US F-5 (3.75 cm);
stitch marker; stitch holder

GAUGE
21 sts and 24 rows = 4" (10 cm)
in Moss stitch

NOTE
Hoodie is worked in one piece,
from Back to Fronts.

STITCH PATTERN
Moss Stitch (multiple of 2 sts + 1; 4-row repeat)
Row 1 (RS): K1, *p1, k1; repeat from * to end.
Rows 2 and 3: P1, *k1, p1; repeat from * to end.
Row 4: Repeat Row 1.
Repeat Rows 1-4 for Moss Stitch.

BODY
Back
CO 47 (51) sts. Begin Moss st. Work even until
piece measures 6 (6½)" [15 (16.5) cm] from the
beginning, ending with a WS row.

Sleeves

Shape Sleeves (RS): Using Cable CO (see Special Techniques, page 158), CO 34 (38) sts at beginning of next 2 rows, working CO sts in Moss st—115 (127) sts. Work even until Sleeves measure 3¼ (3¾)" [8.5 (9.5) cm] from Sleeve CO edge, ending with a WS row.

Shape Neck (RS): Work 47 (52) sts, transfer center 21 (23) sts to st holder for Back neck, join a second ball of yarn, work to end. Working both sides at the same time, work even for 5 rows.

Next Row (RS): Using Cable CO, CO 12 (13) sts at each neck edge once—59 (65) sts each side. Work even until Sleeve measures 6½ (7½)" [16.5 (19) cm] from Sleeve CO edge, ending with a WS row.

Fronts

Next Row (RS): BO 34 (38) sts at beginning of next 2 rows—25 (27) sts remain. Work even until piece measures 6 (6½)" [15 (16.5) cm] from end of Sleeves, ending with a WS row. BO all sts in pattern.

FINISHING

Block piece to measurements.

Hood: With RS facing, pick up and knit 22 (23) sts along Right Front neck edge, work in Moss st across Back neck sts from holder increasing 4 (2) sts across these sts, pick up and knit 22 (23)sts along Left Front neck edge—69 (71) sts. Work even in Moss st until piece measures 6½" [16.5cm] from pick-up row, ending with a WS row. BO all sts in pattern. Fold BO edge of Hood in half and sew halves together. Sew side and Sleeve seams.

Crochet Body Edging: Beginning at left side seam, using crochet hook, ch 3, double crochet (dc) in same st, *skip 1 st, single crochet (sc) in next st, skip 1 st, (2 dc, ch 1, 2 dc) in next st; repeat from * along lower edge, center Front edges, and front of Hood ending with 2 dc, ch 1 in beginning st, join with slip st to top of ch-3. Fasten off.

Crochet Sleeve Edging: Beginning at Sleeve seam, work edging around cuff as for Body.

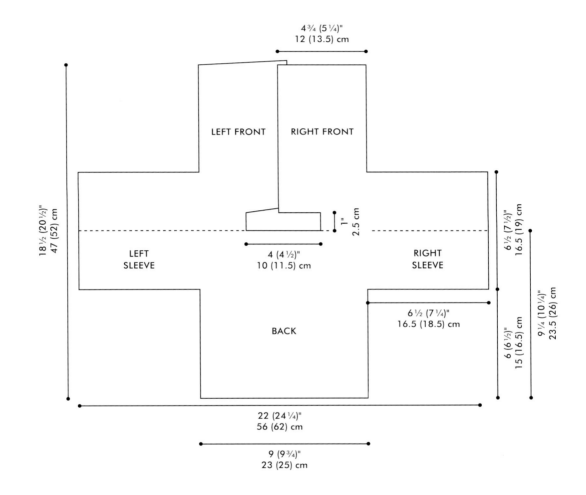

4 ¾ (5 ¼)"
12 (13.5) cm

LEFT FRONT   RIGHT FRONT

1"
2.5 cm

LEFT
SLEEVE

4 (4 ½)"
10 (11.5) cm

RIGHT
SLEEVE

18 ½ (20 ½)"
47 (52) cm

6 ½ (7 ½)"
16.5 (19) cm

9 ¼ (10 ¼)"
23.5 (26) cm

6 ½ (7 ¼)"
16.5 (18.5) cm

BACK

6 (6 ½)"
15 (16.5) cm

22 (24 ¼)"
56 (62) cm

9 (9 ¾)"
23 (25) cm

Milo Soakers

IF YOU ARE USING CLOTH DIAPERS, SOAKERS ARE AS IMPORTANT TODAY AS THEY WERE IN 1943, WHEN THIS PATTERN WAS ORIGINALLY PUBLISHED BY FLEISHER YARNS. THESE ARE SIZED TO FIT OVER A BULKY CLOTH DIAPER; IF YOU'RE PLANNING TO PUT THEM OVER A DISPOSABLE DIAPER, MAKE ONE SIZE SMALLER. I CHOSE STURDY ALL-ORGANIC WOOL COLORED WITH ENVIRONMENTALLY FRIENDLY DYES. BE SURE TO LANOLIZE YOUR SOAKER (SEE THE INSTRUCTIONS ON PAGE 29) IF YOU PLAN TO USE THEM AS A CLOTH DIAPER COVER.

SIZES
3-6 months (6-9 months, 9-12 months, 12-18 months)
Shown in size 6-9 months

FINISHED MEASUREMENTS
16½ (18, 18, 19½)" [42 (46, 46, 50) cm] waist
19 (21, 21, 22½)" [48 (53, 53, 57) cm] hips
8 (9, 10, 11)" [20.5 (23, 25.5, 28) cm] long

YARN
Vermont Organic Fiber Company O-Wool Classic 2-Ply (100% certified organic Merino wool; 198 yards [181 meters] / 50 grams): 1 (1, 1, 2) hanks #4303 Evergreen

NEEDLES
One pair straight needles size US 7 (4.5 mm)
Change needle size if necessary to obtain correct gauge.

GAUGE
20 sts and 40 rows = 4" (10 cm) in Garter st (knit every row)
22 sts and 28 rows = 4" (10 cm) in 2x2 Rib

STITCH PATTERN
2x2 Rib (multiple of 4 sts + 2; 1-row repeat)
Row 1 (RS): K2, *p2, k2; repeat from * to end.
Row 2: Knit the knit sts and purl the purl sts as they face you.
Repeat Row 2 for 2x2 Rib.

SOAKER
Back
CO 46 (50, 50, 54) sts. Begin 2x2 Rib. Work even until piece measures 2" (5 cm) from the beginning, ending with a WS row.
Increase Row (RS): Change to Garter st (knit every row). K1, M1, knit to last st, M1, k1—48 (52, 52, 56) sts.

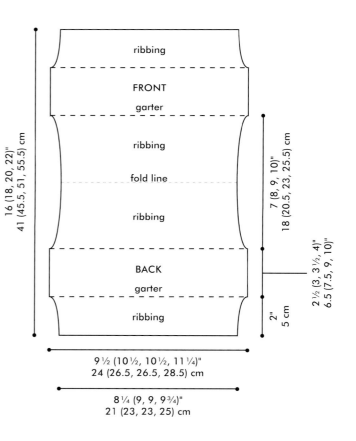

ribbing

FRONT

garter

ribbing

fold line

ribbing

BACK

garter

ribbing

16 (18, 20, 22)"
41 (45.5, 51, 55.5) cm

7 (8, 9, 10)"
18 (20.5, 23, 25.5) cm

2 ½ (3, 3 ½, 4)"
6.5 (7.5, 9, 10)"

2"
5 cm

9 ½ (10 ½, 10 ½, 11 ¼)"
24 (26.5, 26.5, 28.5) cm

8 ¼ (9, 9, 9 ¾)"
21 (23, 23, 25) cm

Work even for 2½ (3, 3½ 4)" [6.5 (7.5, 9, 10) cm], ending with a WS row (piece should measure 4½ (5, 5½, 6)" [11.5 (12.5, 14, 15) cm] from the beginning).

Decrease Row (RS): K1, ssk, knit to last 3 sts, k2tog, k1–46 (50, 50, 54) sts remain.

Legs

Begin Leg Openings (WS): Change to 2x2 Rib. Work even for 7 (8, 9, 10)" [18 (20.5, 23, 25.5) cm], ending with a WS row (piece should measure 11½ (13, 14½, 16)" [29.5 (33, 37, 40.5) cm] from the beginning).

Front

(RS) Repeat Increase Row–48 (52, 52, 56) sts. Work even for 2½ (3, 3½, 4)" [6.5 (7.5, 9, 10) cm], ending with a WS row (piece should measure 14 (16, 18, 20)" [36 (40.5, 46, 50.5) cm] from the beginning).

(RS) Repeat Decrease Row–46 (50, 50, 54) sts remain.

(WS) Change to 2x2 Rib. Work even for 2" (4 cm), ending with a WS row (piece should measure 16 (18, 20, 22)" [41 (45.5, 51, 55.5) cm] from the beginning). BO all sts.

FINISHING

Sew side seams, from waist to leg openings, leaving leg openings unsewn.

The Diaper and the Soaker

In the 1930s, virtually every baby wore cloth diapers—and that meant that every baby wore diaper covers, too. Most mothers preferred practical wool soakers over the other option—sticky, hot rubber pants—because they were soft, absorbent, and breathable. They protected baby's delicate skin from diaper rash and prevented leaks. Even as the disposable diaper was developed in the 1940s and 1950s, most parents still chose dependable cotton diapers with wool soakers.

Today, while disposables are widely available, many parents are again turning to the age-old system of soft cotton cloth diapers paired with hand-knitted wool soakers. With today's new prefolded cotton diapers, this environmentally friendly diapering solution can work even better for us than it did for our grandmothers.

So what's special about wool soakers? The secret is in the fiber. Wool can absorb up to 35 percent of its own weight in liquid and still remain dry to the touch without ever feeling cold or clammy. Even when it is wet, wool stays breathable, helping prevent diaper rash and other discomforts for baby. It also helps maintain normal body temperature—helping baby keep cool in summer and warm in winter. These seemingly contradictory qualities are unique to wool, and unmatched by any synthetic material.

If a wool soaker is intended to be used as a diaper cover, you will want to lanolize the wool by replacing the lanolin it lost during the spinning process. Lanolin creates an effective moisture barrier on the outside of each fiber, allowing a lanolized wool soaker to be waterproof on the outside, yet absorbent. To lanolize your soaker, stir 2 teaspoons pure lanolin (available at any pharmacy) into 2 cups hot water, then immerse your soaker in this solution for 15 minutes, being careful not to agitate too much so it doesn't felt. Lift the soakers gently out of the solution, roll them in a towel to absorb the excess moisture, then dry them flat. Rewash and relanolize soakers when they are soiled or when the lanolin wears out, generally every few weeks.

Stella Pixie Hat

IN THE 1940S AND 1950S POINTY "PIXIE" HATS WERE ALL THE RAGE FOR BABIES.
FOR THIS 1944 VERSION, A KNITTED RECTANGLE IS FOLDED IN HALF AND GRAFTED TOGETHER, THEN
A STRAP IS ADDED ALONG THE BOTTOM TO SECURE THE HAT FIRMLY ON BABY'S HEAD.
I SELECTED A SOFT, SPRINGY WOOL SOCK YARN FOR THIS PROJECT. I OFTEN CHOOSE SOCK YARN FOR
BABY CLOTHES BECAUSE IT IS DURABLE, WASHABLE, AND SOFT, AND BECAUSE IT KNITS UP IN
THE FINER GAUGES THAT ARE SO COMMON IN VINTAGE PATTERNS.

SIZES
3-12 (12-24) months
Shown in size 3-12 months

FINISHED MEASUREMENTS
Approximately 13 (13¾)" [33 (35) cm]
at base of neck, buttoned
8¾ (9½)" [22 (24) cm] to highest point,
at back of Hat
*Note: Choose the appropriate size based
on the height of the Hat. You can adjust the
fit of the neckband if necessary.*

YARN
Blue Moon Fiber Arts Socks that Rock
Mediumweight (100% superwash Merino
wool; 380 yards [347 meters] / 155
grams): 1 hank Coral

NEEDLES
One pair straight needles size
US 3 (3.25 mm)
Spare needle size US 3 (3.25 mm)
or smaller, for Kitchener Stitch
Change needle size if necessary to obtain
correct gauge.

NOTIONS
One ¹¹⁄₁₆" (15 mm) button

GAUGE
36 sts and 36 rows = 4" (10 cm) in 2x2 Rib

NOTES
This Hat is very easy to size up or down
from the sizes given. Simply add or subtract
sts in a multiple of 4 and work the crosswise
ridges as instructed until you have only 2
sts in ribbing at the center of the Hat. Then
complete the Hat as instructed. When
sizing, keep in mind that for every 4 sts you
add or subtract, you will also add or
subtract ⅓" (8 mm) to the height of the Hat,
in order to complete the crosswise ridges.

STITCH PATTERNS
2x2 Rib (multiple of 4 sts + 2; 1-row repeat)
Row 1 (RS): K2, *p2, k2; repeat from * to end.
Row 2: Knit the knit sts and purl the purl sts
as they face you.
Repeat Row 2 for 2x2 Rib.

1x1 Rib (multiple of 2 sts; 1-row repeat)
All Rows: *K1, p1; repeat from * to end.

HAT

CO 98 (106) sts. Begin 2x2 Rib. Work even for 4 rows.

Shape Hat

Row 1 (RS): K6, work in 2x2 Rib to last 6 sts, knit to end.

Row 2: Knit the knit sts and purl the purl sts as they face you.

Row 3: Repeat Row 1.

Row 4: K8, work to last 8 sts, knit to end.

Row 5: Repeat Row 2.

Row 6: Repeat Row 4.

Row 7: K10, work to last 10 sts, knit to end.

Row 8: Repeat Row 2.

Row 9: Repeat Row 7.

Row 10: K12, work to last 12 sts, knit to end.

Row 11: Repeat Row 2.

Row 12: Repeat Row 10.

Row 13: K14, work to last 14 sts, knit to end.

Row 14: Repeat Row 2.

Row 15: Repeat Row 13.

Row 16: K16, work to last 16 sts, knit to end.

Row 17: Repeat Row 2.

Row 18: Repeat Row 16.

Note: You are creating "crosswise ridges" of 3 rows of St st, alternating with 3 rows of Reverse St st, at the beginning and end of every row, with the 2x2 Rib continuing in the center.

Rows 19–64 (70): Continue until 2 sts remain in the 2x2 Rib in the center of the Hat, increasing the number of knit sts worked at the beginning and end of every third row by 2, decreasing the number of 2x2 Rib sts worked in the center of the Hat by 2 on each side, and working all intervening rows by knitting the knit sts and purling the purl sts. Break yarn.

Transfer first 49 (53) sts to spare needle, with point facing towards center of work. Using Kitchener Stitch (see Special Techniques, page 158), graft sts together, beginning at center of work.

Neckband: CO 10 sts. Begin 1x1 Rib. Work even until piece measures 12 (12¾)" [30.5 (32.5) cm] from the beginning, or to 3¾" (9.5 cm) less than desired length.

Make Buttonhole

Row 1 (RS): Work 4 sts, k1-f/b, p1, pass second st on right-hand needle over last st, k1-f/b, pass third st on right-hand needle over last 2 sts, work to end.

Row 2: Work 3 sts, p2tog, turn, CO 4 sts using Cable CO (see Special Techniques, page 158), turn, k2tog, work to end.

Row 3: Work 3 sts, p2tog, k2, p1, k1, p2tog, work to end.

*Work even for 7 rows. Repeat Buttonhole Rows. Repeat from * once. Work even until piece measures 15¾ (16½)" [40 (42) cm] from the beginning, ending with a WS row. BO all sts in pattern.

FINISHING

Block pieces lightly. Sew side edge of Neckband to CO edge of Hat, beginning with CO edge of Neckband flush with right edge of Hat. Sew button to Neckband, so that when fastened, Neckband fits comfortably around neck.

Rufus Textured Cardigan

FEW OF THE OLD PATTERN BOOKLETS I FOUND FROM OUTSIDE OF THE UNITED STATES INCLUDED A PUBLICATION DATE, BUT THIS NEW ZEALAND BOOKLET PLACED ITSELF FIRMLY IN THE 1950S BY DECLARING THIS RAGLAN CARDIGAN TO BE "DESIGNED FOR TV KNITTING." ITS SIMPLE STITCH PATTERN IS INDEED EASY TO MEMORIZE, AND, KNIT UP IN A DK-WEIGHT YARN, IT'S A SNAP TO FINISH. IT IS WORKED IN SEPARATE PIECES, SO YOU DO HAVE SEAMS TO SEW AT THE END – BUT, FORTUNATELY, THE STITCH PATTERN EFFECTIVELY HIDES ANY IMPERFECTIONS IN THE SEAMING. BE SURE TO SECURE THE BUTTONS VERY TIGHTLY TO MAKE SURE THAT BABY CAN'T PULL THEM OFF.

SIZES
3-6 months (6-12 months, 12-18 months)
Shown in size 3-6 months

FINISHED MEASUREMENTS
20 ½ (21 ½, 22 ½)" [52 (54.5, 57) cm]
chest, buttoned

YARN
RYC Cashsoft DK (57% extra fine Merino / 33% microfiber / 10% cashmere; 142 yards [130 meters] / 50 grams): 3 (4, 5) balls #525 Kingfisher

NEEDLES
One pair straight needles size US 4 (3.5 mm)
One pair straight needles size US 5 (3.75 mm)
Change needle size if necessary to obtain correct gauge.

NOTIONS
Stitch holders; five ¾" (20 mm) buttons

GAUGE
24 sts and 40 rows = 4" (10 cm) in Texture Stitch, using larger needles

STITCH PATTERNS
Texture Stitch (multiple of 2 sts + 1; 6-row repeat)
Rows 1 and 3 (RS): P1, *k1, p1; repeat from * to end.
Rows 2, 4, and 5: Purl.
Row 6: Knit.
Repeat Rows 1-6 for Texture Stitch.

1x1 Rib (multiple of 2 sts; 1-row repeat)
Row 1 (RS): *K1, p1; repeat from * to end [end k1 if an odd number of sts].
Row 2: Knit the knit sts and purl the purl sts as they face you.
Repeat Row 2 for 1x1 Rib.

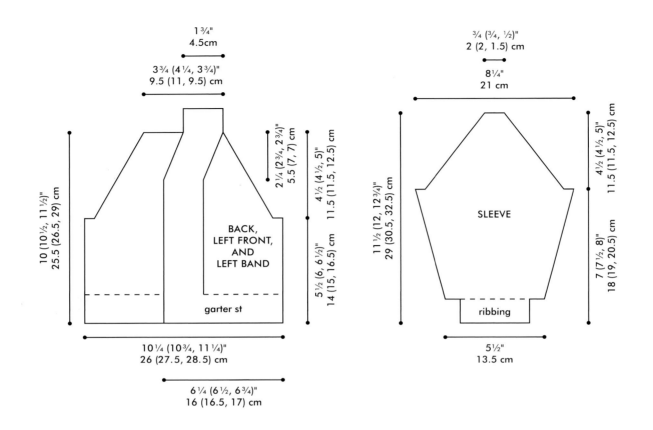

1 ¾"
4.5cm

3 ¾ (4 ¼, 3 ¾)"
9.5 (11, 9.5) cm

2 ¼ (2 ¾, 2 ¾)"
5.5 (7, 7) cm

4 ½ (4 ½, 5)"
11.5 (11.5, 12.5) cm

10 (10 ½, 11 ½)"
25.5 (26.5, 29) cm

5 ½ (6, 6 ½)"
14 (15, 16.5) cm

BACK,
LEFT FRONT,
AND
LEFT BAND

garter st

10 ¼ (10 ¾, 11 ¼)"
26 (27.5, 28.5) cm

6 ¼ (6 ½, 6 ¾)"
16 (16.5, 17) cm

¾ (¾, ½)"
2 (2, 1.5) cm

8 ¼"
21 cm

4 ½ (4 ½, 5)"
11.5 (11.5, 12.5) cm

11 ½ (12, 12 ¾)"
29 (30.5, 32.5) cm

SLEEVE

7 (7 ½, 8)"
18 (19, 20.5) cm

ribbing

5 ½"
13.5 cm

BACK

Using smaller needles, CO 59 (63, 65) sts. Begin Garter st (knit every row). Work even until piece measures 1½" (4 cm) from the beginning, increase 1 st each side on last row–61 (65, 67) sts.
Begin Pattern (RS): Change to larger needles and Texture st. Work even until piece measures 5½ (6, 6½)" [14 (15, 16.5) cm] from the beginning, ending with a WS row.

Shape Raglan Armholes (RS): BO 2 sts at beginning of next 2 rows, decrease 1 st each side every 4 rows 4 times, then every other row 13 (14, 16) times–23 (25, 23) sts remain. BO all sts.

LEFT FRONT

Using smaller needles, CO 37 (39, 41) sts. Begin Garter st.
Girl's Cardigan: Work even for 22 rows.
Boy's Cardigan: Work even for 2 rows.

Boy's Buttonhole (RS): Work buttonhole this row, then every 18 rows once, as follows: Work to last 6 sts, [yo] twice, k2tog, k4.
Next Row (WS): Knit, dropping second yo.

Girl's or Boy's Cardigan:
Begin Pattern (RS): Change to larger needles. Work Texture st to last 10 sts, slip these 10 sts to st holder for Front Band. Working on remaining 27 (29, 31) sts, work even until piece measures 5½ (6, 6½)" [14 (15, 16.5) cm] from the beginning, ending with a WS row.

Shape Raglan Armhole and Neck (RS): BO 2 sts at beginning of next row, decrease 1 st at armhole edge every 4 rows 4 times, then every other row 13 (14, 16) times. AT THE SAME TIME, when 20 (22, 24) sts remain, decrease 1 st at neck edge on next RS row, then every 4 rows 5 (6, 6) times–2 sts remain. Work even for 1 row.
Next Row (RS): K2tog. Fasten off.

RIGHT FRONT

Boy's Cardigan: Work as for Left Front, reversing shaping and stitch patterns, and omitting buttonholes.

Girl's Cardigan: Work as for Left Front, reversing shaping and stitch patterns, and working buttonholes on same rows as Left Front, Boy's Cardigan, as follows:

Girl's Buttonhole (RS): K5, [yo] twice, k2tog, work to end.

Next Row: Knit, dropping second yo.

SLEEVES

Using smaller needles, CO 32 sts. Begin 1x1 Rib. Work even until piece measures 1¼" (3 cm) from the beginning, increase 1 st at end of last (WS) row–33 sts.

Begin Pattern (RS): Change to larger needles and Texture st. Work even for 2 rows.

Shape Sleeve (RS): Increase 1 st each side this row, then every 6 rows 7 times, working increased sts in Texture st as they become available–49 sts. Work even until piece measures 7 (7½, 8)" [18 (19, 20.5) cm] from the beginning, or to desired length, ending with a WS row.

Shape Cap (RS): BO 2 sts at beginning of next 2 rows, decrease 1 st each side every 4 rows 1 (2, 3) times, then every other row 19 (18, 18) times–5 (5, 3) sts remain. BO all sts.

FINISHING

Block pieces to measurements. Sew raglan seams. Sew side and Sleeve seams.

Left Front Band (RS): Rejoin yarn to sts on holder for Left Front. Using smaller needles, work in Garter st to end.

Girl's Cardigan: Work even until Band is long enough to fit up Front edge and halfway across Back neck. BO all sts.

Boy's Cardigan: Work even for 17 rows.

Next Row (RS): Work Boy's Buttonhole this row, then every 18 rows twice. Finish as for Girl's Cardigan.

Right Front Band: Rejoin yarn to sts on holder for Right Front. Using smaller needles, work in Garter st to end.

Boy's Cardigan: Work as for Left Front Band, omitting buttonholes.

Girl's Cardigan: Work even for 17 rows.

Next Row (RS): Work Girl's Buttonhole this row, then every 18 rows twice. Complete as for Left Front Band.

Sew Bands to Front edges and Back neck.

Sew BO edges together at center Back neck. Sew on buttons opposite buttonholes.

Louise Cardigan

THE SELECTION OF NEW YARNS AND PATTERNS AVAILABLE TO THE AVERAGE AMERICAN CONSUMER EXPLODED
DURING THE KNITTING CRAZE OF THE 1930S, AND AGAIN IN THE POSTWAR YEARS. ONE OF THE MANY
INTRODUCTIONS TO THE MARKET INCLUDED QUICK-TO-KNIT YARNS FOR BUSY OR IMPATIENT KNITTERS. COLUMBIA
YARNS MARKETED THEIR PRODUCTS AS "JIFFY KNITS," PUBLISHING ENTIRE BOOKS DEVOTED TO PATTERNS FOR THEIR
NEW HEAVIER GAUGE YARNS. THIS 1950S RAGLAN SWEATER IS INDEED EASY TO FINISH AND LOOKS
SOPHISTICATED ON EVEN THE TINIEST BABY. I CHOSE A VERY SOFT AUSTRALIAN WOOL YARN AND LITTLE RED BAKELITE
BUTTONS TO HIGHLIGHT THE YARN'S WONDERFUL STRAWBERRY-COLORED FLECKS. WHEN YOU SEW ON YOUR
BUTTONS, MAKE SURE THAT THEY ARE SECURED VERY TIGHTLY FOR BABY'S SAFETY.

SIZES
0-3 months
(3-6 months, 6-9 months, 9-12 months)
Shown in size 0-3 months

FINISHED MEASUREMENTS
21½ (22¼, 23½, 24½)"
[54.5 (56.5, 59.5, 62) cm] chest

YARN
Pear Tree 4-ply Merino
(100% Australian Merino wool;
175 yards [160 meters] / 50 grams):
2 (3, 3, 3) hanks Blush

NEEDLES
One pair straight needles size US 3 (3.25 mm)
One 24" (60 cm) long circular (circ)
needle size US 3 (3.25 mm)
Change needle size if necessary to
obtain correct gauge.

NOTIONS
Stitch markers; stitch holders or waste yarn;
two ½" (13 mm) buttons

GAUGE
27 sts and 38 rows = 4" (10 cm)
in Stockinette st (St st)

NOTES
The Body is worked back and forth in one
piece to the armholes, then set aside. The
Sleeves are also worked to the armholes,
then set aside. The Body and Sleeves are
then joined at the armholes, and the Yoke
is worked back and forth to the end.

STITCH PATTERNS

Seed Stitch (odd number of sts; 1-row repeat)
All Rows: *K1, p1; repeat from * to last st, k1.

Slip Stitch Pattern
(multiple of 3 sts + 2; 4-row repeat)
Row 1 (RS): K1, *slip 1 wyif, yo, k2, psso (passing slipped stitch over yo and k2); repeat from * to last st, k1.
Row 2: Purl.
Row 3: K2, *slip 1 wyif, yo, k2, psso; repeat from * to end.
Row 4: Purl.
Repeat Rows 1-4 for Slip Stitch Pattern.

BODY

Using circ needle, CO 41 (42, 44, 45) sts for Right Front, place marker (pm), CO 75 (79, 83, 87) sts for Back, pm, CO 41 (42, 44, 45) sts for Left Front—157 (163, 171, 177) sts. Do not join. Begin Seed st; work even for 6 rows.
Next Row (RS): Work 5 sts in Seed st, work in St st to last 5 sts, work in Seed st to end. Work even for 5 rows.
Next Row (RS): Change to Seed st across all sts. Work even for 5 rows.
Next Row (RS): Work 5 sts in Seed st, work in St st to last 5 sts, work in Seed st to end. Work even for 1 row.

Shape Body (RS): Decrease 4 sts this row, then every 8 (10, 12, 16) rows twice, as follows: [Work to 2 sts before marker, k2tog, slip marker (sm), ssk] twice, work to end—145 (151, 159, 165) sts remain. Work even for 5 (7, 7, 5) rows.
Shape Armholes (RS): [Work to 4 sts before marker, BO 8 sts for underarm, removing marker] twice, work to end—129 (135, 143, 149) sts remain [34 (35, 37, 38) sts each Front; 61 (65, 69, 73) sts for Back]. Place sts on st holder or waste yarn. Do not break yarn.

SLEEVES

With straight needles, CO 27 (31, 33, 35) sts; begin Seed st. Work even for 11 rows, increase 8 (7, 8, 9) sts evenly spaced across last row—35 (38, 41, 44) sts. Knit 1 row.
Next Row (RS): Change to Slip Stitch Pattern. Work even for 4 rows. Purl 2 rows.
Shape Sleeve (RS): Change to St st, increase 1 st each side this row, every other row 2 (0, 0, 0) times, every 4 rows 3 (5, 2, 0) times, then every 6 rows 0 (0, 3, 5) times, as follows: K1, M1, work to last st, M1, k1—47 (50, 53, 56) sts. Work even for 3 (5, 3, 5) rows. Work even until piece measures 4½ (5, 5½, 6)" [11.5 (12.5, 14, 15) cm] from the beginning ending with a WS row.
Shape Cap (RS): Bind off 4 sts at beginning of next 2 rows—39 (42, 45, 48) sts remain. Break yarn, leaving a 12" tail, and place all sts on st holder or waste yarn.

YOKE

Join Body and Sleeves (WS): Transfer Body sts to circ needle. With WS facing, using yarn attached to Body, and continuing in pattern as established, work across 34 (35, 37, 38) sts for Left Front, pm, 39 (42, 45, 48) sts from holder for Left Sleeve, pm, 61 (65, 69, 73) sts for Back, pm, 39 (42, 45, 48) sts from holder for Right Sleeve, pm, 34 (35, 37, 38) sts for Right Front—207 (219, 233, 245) sts.

Shape Raglan
Row 1 (RS): [Work to 2 sts before marker, k2tog, sm, ssk] 4 times, work to end—199 (211, 225, 237) sts remain.
Row 2: Work even.
Row 3: [Work to 2 sts before marker, k2tog, sm, work to next marker, sm, ssk] twice, work to end—195 (207, 221, 233) sts remain.
Row 4: Work even.
Rows 5-16 (16, 20, 16): Repeat Rows 1-4—159 (171, 173, 197) sts remain after Row 15 (15, 19, 15).

SIZES 0-3 MONTHS AND 3-6 MONTHS ONLY
Rows 17 and 18: Repeat Rows 1 and 2—151 (163) sts remain.
Row 19: *Work to 2 sts before marker, k2tog, sm, work to next marker, sm, ssk), [k13 (15), k2tog] twice; repeat from * once, work to end—145 (157) sts remain.
Row 20 (WS): Work 5 sts, k2tog, knit to last 5 sts, work to end—144 (156) sts remain.

SIZE 6-9 MONTHS ONLY
Row 21: Work to second marker, sm, k24, k2tog, work to end—172 sts remain.
Row 22 (WS): Work 5 sts, k2tog, knit to last 5 sts, work to end—171 sts remain.

SIZE 9-12 MONTHS ONLY
Rows 17, 18, 20-22, and 24: Work even.
Row 19: Repeat Row 1—189 sts remain.
Row 23: Repeat Row 3—185 sts remain.
Row 25: Work to second marker, sm, k26, k2tog, work to end—184 sts remain.
Row 26 (WS): Work 5 sts, k2tog, knit to last 5 sts, work to end—183 sts remain.

ALL SIZES
Begin Yoke Pattern
Row 1 (RS): Work 5 sts in Seed st, work in Slip Stitch Pattern to last 5 sts, work in Seed st to end.
Row 2: Work even.
Row 3 (Buttonhole Row): K1, p2tog, yo, p1, k1, work to end.

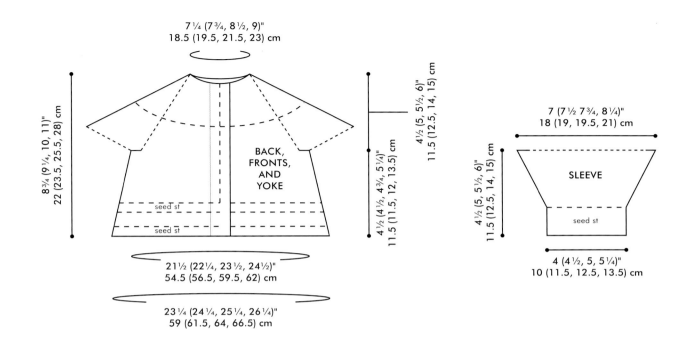

7 ¼ (7 ¾, 8 ½, 9)"
18.5 (19.5, 21.5, 23) cm

8 ¾ (9 ¼, 10, 11)"
22 (23.5, 25.5, 28) cm

BACK,
FRONTS,
AND
YOKE

seed st

seed st

4 ½ (5, 5 ½, 6)"
11.5 (12.5, 14, 15) cm

4 ½ (4 ½, 4 ¾, 5 ¼)"
11.5 (11.5, 12, 13.5) cm

21 ½ (22 ¼, 23 ½, 24 ½)"
54.5 (56.5, 59.5, 62) cm

23 ¼ (24 ¼, 25 ¼, 26 ¼)"
59 (61.5, 64, 66.5) cm

7 (7 ½, 7 ¾, 8 ¼)"
18 (19, 19.5, 21) cm

SLEEVE

seed st

4 ½ (5, 5 ½, 6)"
11.5 (12.5, 14, 15) cm

4 (4 ½, 5, 5 ¼)"
10 (11.5, 12.5, 13.5) cm

Row 4: Work even.

Row 5: Work 5 sts in Seed st, p6, *p2tog, p2; repeat from * to last 9 (9, 8, 8) sts, p4 (2, 3, 6), [p2tog] 0 (1, 0, 1) time(s), work to end—113 (121, 133, 141) sts remain.

Row 6: Work 5 sts in Seed st, purl to last 5 sts, work in Seed st to end.

Row 7: Work 5 sts in Seed st, knit to last 5 sts, work in Seed st to end.

Row 8: Change to Seed st across all sts.

Row 9: Work even.

Row 10: Work 5 sts in Seed st, purl to last 5 sts, work in Seed st to end.

Row 11: Repeat Row 7.

Row 12: Work 5 sts in Seed st, k2, *k2tog, k2; repeat from * to last 6 sts, k1, work in Seed st to end—88 (94, 103, 109) sts remain.

Rows 13-16: Repeat Rows 1-4.

Row 17: Work 5 sts in Seed st, *p2tog; repeat from * to last 5 (5, 6, 6) sts, k0 (0, 1, 1), work in Seed st to end—49 (52, 57, 60) sts remain.

Rows 18 and 20: Purl.

Row 19: Knit.

Row 21 (Picot Turning Row): K1 (2, 1, 2), *yo, k2tog; rep from * to end.

Row 22: Purl.

Row 23: Knit.

BO all sts loosely purlwise.

FINISHING

With damp cloth and warm iron, press lightly. Using long tails at underarms, sew underarm seams. Sew Sleeve seams. Turn BO edge of Yoke to WS at Picot Turning Row and sew to WS, being careful not to let sts show on RS. Sew on buttons opposite buttonholes. Press all seams.

Liza Sideways Sacque

THE INTERESTING CONSTRUCTION OF THIS 1920S CARDIGAN MAKES IT FUN TO KNIT. FIRST,
THE BODY OF THE CARDIGAN IS WORKED FROM SIDE TO SIDE INSTEAD OF THE USUAL BOTTOM UP, THEN
STITCHES ARE PICKED UP ALONG THE BOTTOM EDGE TO CREATE A HEM AND ALONG THE TOP EDGE TO
CREATE A YOKED COLLAR. THE SLEEVES ARE ALSO WORKED FROM SIDE TO SIDE, WITH STITCHES PICKED UP ALONG
THE BOTTOMS FOR CUFFS. REMEMBER, GARMENTS WITH RIBBONS SHOULD ONLY BE WORN
WHEN BABY IS SUPERVISED. IF YOU PREFER, LEAVE THE RIBBONS OFF AND LET BABY WEAR THE SWEATER OPEN.

SIZES
12-18 months (18-24 months)
Shown in size 12-18 months

FINISHED MEASUREMENTS
20½ (25)" [51 (63.5) cm] chest

YARN
Dale of Norway Baby Ull (100% superwash
Merino wool; 192 yards [175 meters] / 50
grams): 1 (2) skeins #2106 Sunny Yellow
(MC); 2 (2) skeins #0010 White (A)

NEEDLES
One pair straight needles size
US 1 (2.25 mm)
One pair straight needles size
US 3 (3.25 mm)
Change needle size if necessary to
obtain correct gauge.

NOTIONS
4 yards (4 meters) ⅜" (1 cm) wide
satin ribbon

GAUGE
24 sts and 53 rows = 4" (10 cm) in Garter
Eyelet Pattern, using larger needles

STITCH PATTERN
**Garter Eyelet Pattern (odd number of sts;
16-row repeat)**
Row 1 (RS): With MC, knit.
Rows 2-10: Work in Garter st (knit every row).
Row 11: Change to A. Knit.
Row 12: Purl.
Row 13: Slip 1 st, *yo, k2tog; repeat from
* to end.
Rows 14 and 15: Knit.
Row 16: Purl.
Repeat Rows 1-16 for Garter Eyelet Pattern.

BODY
Right Front
Using larger needles and MC, CO 41 (45) sts.
Begin Garter Eyelet Pattern. Work even for
50 (52) rows.
Shape Shoulder (RS): Using Cable CO
(see Special Techniques, page 158), CO 12 sts
for shoulder, work to end–53 (57) sts. Work
even for 15 (29) rows.
Shape Armhole (RS): BO 20 (22) sts, work to
end–33 (35) sts remain.
Next Row (WS): Work to last 3 sts, k2tog,
k1–32 (34) sts remain. Work even for 1 row.

Back
(WS) Work to last st, M1, k1–33 (35) sts remain.
Next Row (RS): Using Cable CO, CO 20 (22) sts,
work to end–53 (57) sts. Work even for 15 (29) rows.
Shape Right Shoulder (RS): BO 12 sts, work
to end–41 (45) sts remain. Work even for 97
(101) rows.

knitting in the 1920s

Things looked good for knitting at the start of the 1920s. At the end of World War I, yarn companies introduced a slew of new yarns and patterns in an attempt to entice the millions of wartime charity knitters who could now turn their needles to more peaceful projects.

But hard times were ahead for the knitting industry. While knitting had reached new heights of popularity during the war, it fell out of fashion as the 1920s wore on. The rise of youth culture and the politics of women's liberation among the flapper generation did not bode well for such "women's work." Postwar prosperity and readily available commercially knit garments made knitting less of a necessity. And the number of hand-knitted styles in fashion design decreased precipitously. While the long, boxy sweater was a staple in every flapper's wardrobe, gone were the intricate shawls and bed jackets of the previous generation.

Knitting companies sought to rekindle the craze for knitting, and hosted contests and knitting marathons throughout the decade. But articles on knitting in magazines and newspapers dwindled as the decade progressed, and soon the only newpaper articles on knitting told stories of mill and shop closures and price cuts on yarn.

Knitting for baby, however, was still deemed essential, and yarn companies like Bear-Bucilla and Fleisher's published dozens of pattern books for youngsters. The fashion for babies in the 1920s reflected adult trends at the time, featuring long, drop-waisted sweaters and tunics, often with simple stitch patterns and squared collars or boat necks. The layette set, usually consisting of a blanket with matching sweater, booties, and hat, was also popular.

By the time of the stock market crash in 1929, the knitting industry had reached a new low. But while hard times were ahead for virtually everyone, knitting—a cheap and practical way to both clothe and entertain oneself—saw its prospects soar.

Shape Left Shoulder (RS): Using Cable CO, CO 12 sts for shoulder, work to end–53 (57) sts. Work even for 15 (29) rows.
Shape Armhole (RS): BO 20 (22) sts, work to end–33 (35) sts remain.
Next Row (WS): Work to last 3 sts, k2tog, k1–32 (34) sts remain. Work even for 1 row.

Left Front
(WS) Work to last st, M1, k1–33 (35) sts remain.
Next Row (RS): Using Cable CO, CO 20 (22) sts, work to end–53 (57) sts. Work even for 15 (29) rows.
Shape Shoulder (RS): BO 12 sts, work to end–41 (45) sts remain. Work even for 51 (53) rows.
BO all sts.

Sleeves
Using larger needles and MC, CO 30 (34) sts.
Shape Sleeve
Increase Row (RS): Begin Garter Eyelet Pattern. Increase 1 st this row, then every other row 4 (6) times, as follows: K1, M1, work to end–35 (41) sts. Work even for 61 (69) rows.
Decrease Row (RS): Decrease 1 st this row, then every other row 4 (6) times, as follows: K1, k2tog, work to end–30 (34) sts remain. Work even for 1 row. BO all sts.

Cuffs
Using larger needles and A, pick up and knit 5 sts in each MC stripe and 2 sts in each A stripe along left edge of Sleeve, adjusting as necessary to end with a multiple of 3 sts.
Rows 1-9: Work in Garter st.
Rows 10-13: Change to smaller needles. Work in St st.
Row 14: *K1, [yo] twice, k2tog; repeat from * to end.
Row 15: *P1, k1, dropping second yo, p1; repeat from * to end.
Rows 16-19: Repeat Rows 10-13.

Fold hem to WS at Row 14. Using Kitchener st (see Special Techniques, page 158), graft hem to WS at Row 10. *Note: If you prefer, you may BO all sts after Row 19, and sew hem to WS rather than grafting; make sure sts do not show on RS.*

FINISHING

Sew shoulder seams. Set in Sleeves. Sew Sleeve seams.

Bottom Band: Using larger needles and A, pick up and knit 5 sts in each MC stripe and 3 sts in each A stripe along entire lower edge, adjusting as necessary to end with a multiple of 3 sts.

Row 1 (WS): Purl.

Row 2: *K1, [yo] twice, k2tog; repeat from * to end.

Row 3: *P1, k1, dropping second yo, p1; repeat from * to end.

Rows 4-19: Work in Garter st.

Rows 20-23: Change to smaller needles. Work in St st.

Rows 24 and 25: Repeat Rows 2 and 3.

Rows 26-29: Repeat Rows 20-23.

Fold hem to WS at Row 24. Using Kitchener st, graft hem to Row 19. *Note: If you prefer, you may BO all sts after Row 29, and sew hem to WS rather than grafting; make sure sts do not show on RS.*

Yoke

With RS facing, using larger needles and A, pick up and knit 5 sts in each MC stripe and 2 sts in each A stripe along Right Front neck edge, place marker (pm), 1 st in corner, 1 st for each st CO for shoulders, 1 st in corner, pm, 5 sts in each MC stripe and 2 sts in each A stripe along Back neck edge, pm, 1 st in corner, 1 st for each st CO for shoulders, 1 st in corner, pm, and 5 sts in each MC stripe and 2 sts in each A stripe along Left Front neck edge, adjusting as necessary to end with a multiple of 3 sts.

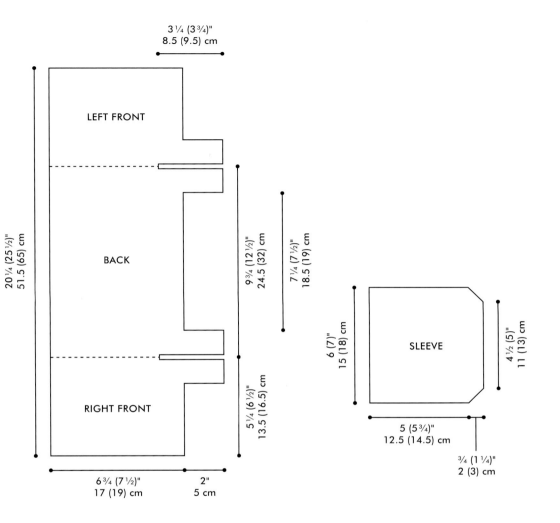

Rows 1-9: Working in Garter st, [work to marker, slip marker (sm), k2tog, work to 2 sts before next marker, k2tog, sm] twice, work to end.

Row 10: *K1, [yo] twice, k2tog; repeat from * to end.

Row 11: *P1, k1, dropping second yo, p1; repeat from * to end.

Rows 12-15: Change to smaller needles. Work in St st.

Rows 16-21: Repeat Rows 10-15.

Fold hem to WS at Row 16. Using Kitchener st, graft hem to WS at Row 12. *Note: If you prefer, you may BO all sts after Row 21, and sew hem to WS rather than grafting; make sure sts do not show on RS.*

Jasper Diamond Hoodie

TAKEN FROM A 1950 PATTERN BOOKLET, THIS CARDIGAN HOODIE LOOKS EQUALLY
GOOD ON A BOY OR A GIRL. IT IS WORKED IN ONE PIECE TO THE ARMHOLES, THEN THE DIFFERENT
PARTS (FRONTS, BACK, AND SLEEVES) ARE WORKED SEPARATELY BEFORE STITCHES ARE PICKED UP AROUND
THE NECK AND SHOULDERS FOR THE HOOD. I CHOSE TO MAKE THIS SWEATER WITH BAMBOO
YARN, A MODERN CHOICE OF WHICH I'M SURE OUR GRANDMOTHERS WOULD APPROVE. IT'S SOFT AND
MACHINE-WASHABLE, AND IT DRAPES BEAUTIFULLY. AS WITH ALL PATTERNS THAT USE BUTTONS,
MAKE SURE THEY ARE SECURED VERY TIGHTLY FOR SAFETY'S SAKE.

SIZES
6-9 months (9-12 months,
12-18 months, 18-24 months)
Shown in size 6-9 months

FINISHED MEASUREMENTS
21 (22 ½, 23 ½, 25)" [53.5 (57, 59.5, 63.5)
cm] chest, buttoned

YARN
Sirdar Snuggly Baby Bamboo (80% bamboo
/ 20% wool; 105 yards [96 meters] / 50
grams): 5 (6, 7, 8) balls #140 Minky

NEEDLES
One pair straight needles
size US 4 (3.5 mm)
Change needle size if necessary
to obtain correct gauge.

NOTIONS
One crochet hook size US E-4 (3.5 mm)
(optional); stitch markers; stitch holders;
six ⅝" (16 mm) buttons

GAUGE
24 sts and 32 rows = 4" (10 cm)
in Diamond Pattern

STITCH PATTERNS
Seed Stitch (odd number of sts; 1-row repeat)
All Rows: *K1, p1; repeat from * to last st, k1.

Diamond Pattern (multiple of 8 sts + 1; 16-row repeat) (see Chart)
Row 1 (RS): K1, *k3, p1, k4; repeat from * to end.
Row 2 and all WS rows: Knit the knit sts and
purl the purl sts as they face you.
Row 3: K1, *k2, p1, k1, p1, k3; repeat from * to end.
Row 5: K1, *k1, p1, k3, p1, k2; repeat from * to end.
Row 7: K1, *p1, k5, p1, k1; repeat from * to end.
Row 9: P1, *k7, p1; repeat from * to end.
Row 11: Repeat Row 7.
Row 13: Repeat Row 5.
Row 15: Repeat Row 3.
Row 16: Knit the knit sts and purl the purl sts
as they face you.
Repeat Rows 1–16 for Diamond Pattern.

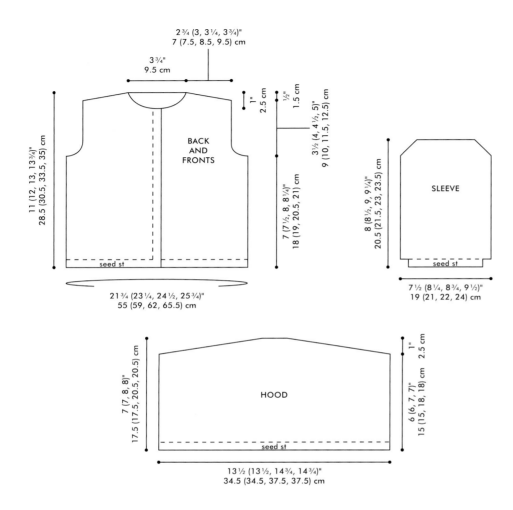

Measurements on diagram:

2 ¾ (3, 3 ¼, 3 ¾)"
7 (7.5, 8.5, 9.5) cm

3 ¾"
9.5 cm

1"
2.5 cm

½"
1.5 cm

9 (10, 11.5, 12.5) cm
3 ½ (4, 4 ½, 5)"

BACK
AND
FRONTS

11 (12, 13, 13 ¾)"
28.5 (30.5, 33.5, 35) cm

7 (7 ½, 8, 8 ¼)"
18 (19, 20.5, 21) cm

seed st

21 ¾ (23 ¼, 24 ½, 25 ¾)"
55 (59, 62, 65.5) cm

SLEEVE

8 (8 ½, 9, 9 ¼)"
20.5 (21.5, 23, 23.5) cm

seed st

7 ½ (8 ¼, 8 ¾, 9 ½)"
19 (21, 22, 24) cm

HOOD

7 (7, 8, 8)"
17.5 (17.5, 20.5, 20.5) cm

1"
2.5 cm

6 (6, 7, 7)"
15 (15, 18, 18) cm

seed st

13 ½ (13 ½, 14 ¾, 14 ¾)"
34.5 (34.5, 37.5, 37.5) cm

BODY

CO 131 (139, 147, 155) sts. Begin Seed st. Work even for 8 rows.

Work Buttonhole and Begin Pattern (RS): K1, p1, BO 2 sts, k1, place marker (pm), work in Diamond Pattern (you may follow text or Chart for pattern) to last 5 sts, pm, work in Seed st to end.

Next Row: Work in Seed st to first marker, work in Diamond Pattern to next marker, k1, CO 2 sts over buttonhole, p1, k1.

Next Row: Work in Seed st to first marker, work in Diamond Pattern to next marker, work in Seed st to end. Work even until piece measures 7 (7 ½, 8, 8 ¼)" [18 (19, 20.5, 21) cm] from the beginning, ending with a WS row. AT THE SAME TIME, work an additional buttonhole approximately every 1 ¾"; you will have 6 total buttonholes when all shaping is complete.

Shape Armholes (RS): Work 31 (33, 35, 37) sts for Right Front, join second ball of yarn, BO 6 sts for underarm, work 57 (61, 65, 69) sts, transfer these sts to st holder for Back, BO 6 sts, work to end.

Note: Make note of what row number of the Chart you will need to end on the same row when working Sleeves.

FRONTS

Working both Fronts at the same time, work even for 1 row.

Next Row (RS): Decrease 1 st at each armhole edge–30 (32, 34, 36) sts remain for each Front. Work even until Fronts measure 3 (3 ½, 4, 4 ½)" [7.5 (9, 10, 11.5) cm] from beginning of shaping, ending at neck edge.

Shape Neck and Shoulders: BO 10 sts at each neck edge once, then 2 sts at each neck edge every other row twice, and AT THE SAME TIME when armholes measure 3 ½ (4, 4 ½, 5)" [9 (10, 11.5, 12.5) cm] from beginning of shaping, BO 8 (9, 10, 11) sts at armhole edge every other row twice.

BACK

Transfer Back sts to needle. With WS facing, join yarn at armhole edge. Work even for 1 row.

Next Row (RS): Decrease 1 st each side–55 (59, 63, 67) sts remain. Work even until armholes measure 3 ½ (4, 4 ½, 5)" [9 (10, 11.5, 12.5) cm] from beginning of shaping, ending with a WS row.

Shape Shoulders (RS): BO 8 (9, 10, 11) sts at beginning of next 4 rows. BO remaining 23 sts.

SLEEVES

CO 33 (35, 39, 41) sts. Begin Seed st. Work even for 8 rows, increase 12 (14, 14, 16) sts evenly spaced across last row–45 (49, 53, 57) sts.

Begin Pattern (RS): Change to Diamond Pattern from Chart, beginning with st# 7 (1, 7, 1) as indicated in Chart. Work even until piece measures 7 (7 ½, 8, 8 ¼)" [18 (19, 20.5, 21) cm] from the beginning, ending with same row as for Body at underarm.

Shape Cap: BO 3 sts at beginning of next 8 rows. BO remaining 21 (25, 29, 33) sts.

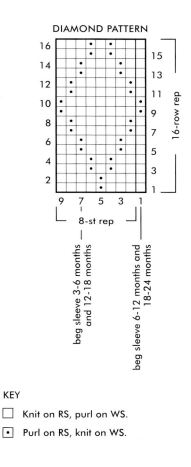

DIAMOND PATTERN

8-st rep

16-row rep

beg sleeve 3-6 months and 12-18 months

beg sleeve 6-12 months and 18-24 months

KEY

☐ Knit on RS, purl on WS.

⊡ Purl on RS, knit on WS.

HOOD

With larger needles, CO 81 (81, 89, 89) sts. Begin Seed st. Work even for 7 rows.

Increase Row (WS): Continuing in Seed st, work 19 (19, 23, 23) sts, [M1, work 6 sts] 8 times, work to end–89, (89, 97, 97) sts.

Begin Pattern (RS): Change to Diamond Pattern. Work even until piece measures 6 (6, 7, 7)" [15 (15, 18, 18) cm] from the beginning, ending with a WS row.

Note: Hood is shaped using short rows (see Special Techniques, page 158).

Work Short Rows (RS): Change to St st. [Work to last 9 sts, wrp-t] twice, [work to 9 sts before wrapped st of row below last row worked, wrp-t] 6 times, work to end of row, working wrapped sts together with wraps as you come to them.

Next Row (WS): Work across all sts, working wraps together with wrapped sts as you come to them.

Next Row: K44 (44, 48, 48) sts, k2tog, knit to end. Break yarn, leaving a 35" (89 cm) or longer tail for grafting.

Fold Hood in half widthwise. Graft live sts together using Kitchener st (see Special Techniques, page 158).

FINISHING

Block pieces to measurements. Sew shoulder seams. Set in Sleeves. Sew Sleeve seams. Sew Hood to neck edge. With crochet hook, work one row single crochet around neck edge of Body and CO edge of Hood (optional), making sure to work same number of single crochet sts on each edge. Sew buttons opposite Buttonholes.

Betty Lou Lace Cardigan

CONSTRUCTED IN ONE PIECE FROM THE TOP DOWN, THIS RAGLAN
FROM A 1944 COLUMBIA YARN COMPANY PATTERN IS AN EXCELLENT EXAMPLE OF A STAPLE
IN THE WARDROBE OF A WORLD WAR II-ERA BABY. WHILE GIRLS AND BOYS ALIKE
WOULD HAVE WORN THIS CARDIGAN, WORKED AS SHOWN HERE IN SOFT PERIWINKLE
BLUE WOOL, IT SEEMS PERFECT FOR A LITTLE GIRL.

SIZES

0–3 months (3–6 months, 6–12 months,
12–18 months)
Shown in size 6–12 months

FINISHED MEASUREMENTS

18 (20¼, 21¾, 24)" [45.5 (51.5, 55, 61)
cm] chest

YARN

Lorna's Laces Shepherd Sock (80% superwash
wool / 20% nylon; 215 yards [196 meters] /
2 ounces [57 grams]): 4 (4, 5, 6) hanks
#049 Periwinkle

NEEDLES

One 24" (60 cm) long or longer circular
(circ) needle size US 2 (2.75 mm)
One pair double-pointed needles
(dpn) size US 2 (2.75 mm)
Change needle size if necessary to
obtain correct gauge.

NOTIONS

Stitch markers; stitch holders; pompom
maker or 2 cardboard circles, each 1"
(2.5 cm) diameter, for Pompoms

GAUGE

32 sts and 36 rows = 4" (10 cm) in
Stockinette stitch (St st)

STITCH PATTERN

Lace Stitch (multiple of 3 sts + 1; 2-row repeat)
Row 1 (RS): *K2tog, yo, k1; repeat from * to last
st, k1.
Row 2: *P2tog, yo, p1; repeat from * to last st, p1.
Repeat Rows 1 and 2 for Lace Stitch.

YOKE

Note: Cardigan is worked from the top down.
Using circ needle, CO 2 sts for Left Front, place
marker (pm), 1 st for raglan "seam", pm, 5 (2, 4,
1) sts for Left sleeve, pm, 1 st for "seam", pm,
20 (26, 24, 30) sts for Back, pm, 1 st for "seam,"
pm, 5 (2, 4, 1) sts for Right Sleeve, pm, 1 st for
"seam", pm, 2 sts for Right Front–38 (38, 40, 40)
sts. Do not join.

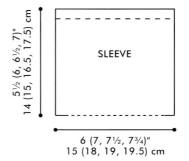

Pink vs. Blue

Most of us in the Western world associate pink with girls and blue with boys. But, despite the fact that these color-gender associations seem set in stone today, they are actually relatively new. Before the 1920s, pink was preferred for boys. As a relative of red, it was thought to be more masculine and aggressive. Blue, which was associated with the Virgin Mary, was considered more dainty and demure, and was, therefore, worn primarily by girls.

Although preferences began to change after World War I, when blue was used extensively in military uniforms, the transformation was gradual. In 1927, when a Belgian infant princess was greeted with a layette of blue, *Time* magazine ran a story about the color of baby clothes in department store by gender. They concluded that there was "no great unanimity of U.S. opinion on Pink v. Blue." In the 1940s, magazines began to push pink as a feminine color and emphasize blue for boys. By the 1950s the codification of pink for girls and blue for boys was complete.

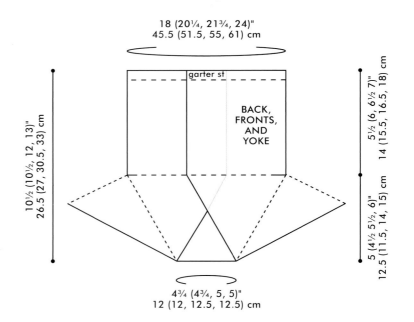

18 (20¼, 21¾, 24)"
45.5 (51.5, 55, 61) cm

garter st

BACK, FRONTS, AND YOKE

10½ (10½, 12, 13)"
26.5 (27, 30.5, 33) cm

5½ (6, 6½, 7)"
14 (15.5, 16.5, 18) cm

5 (4½, 5½, 6)"
12.5 (11.5, 14, 15) cm

4¾ (4¾, 5, 5)"
12 (12, 12.5, 12.5) cm

Note: Pieces are worked from the top down.

SLEEVE

5½ (6, 6½, 7)"
14 (15, 16.5, 17.5) cm

6 (7, 7½, 7¾)"
15 (18, 19, 19.5) cm

Row 1 (RS): K1, M1, [knit to marker, yo, slip marker (sm), k1, sm, yo] 4 times, knit to last st, M1, k1–48 (48, 50, 50) sts.

Row 2: Purl.

Rows 3 and 4: Repeat Rows 1 and 2–58 (58, 60, 60) sts.

Row 5: Repeat Row 1–68 (68, 70, 70) sts.

Row 6: Knit.

Rows 7-10: Repeat Rows 3-6–88 (88, 90, 90) sts after Row 9.

Repeat Rows 1-10 three (3, 3, 4) times, then Rows 1-6 zero (0, 1, 0) time(s)–238 (238, 270, 290) sts [42 (42, 48, 52) sts each Front, 47 (44, 52, 53) sts each Sleeve (including "seam" sts), 60 (66, 70, 80) sts for Back]. Break yarn.

BODY

Next Row (RS): Work to first marker, transfer next 47 (44, 52, 53) sts to st holder for Left Sleeve (including "seam" sts), remove markers, CO 0 (6, 4, 4) sts for underarm, work to next marker, transfer next 47 (44, 52, 53) sts to st holder for Right Sleeve (including "seam" sts), remove markers, CO 0 (6, 4, 4) sts for underarm, work to end–144 (162, 174, 192) sts remain. Purl 1 row, increase 34 (37, 40, 46) sts evenly spaced across row–178 (199, 214, 238) sts.

Next Row (RS): Change to Lace Stitch. Work even until piece measures 5 (5½, 6, 6½)" [12.5 (14, 15, 16.5) cm] from underarm, ending with a WS row.

Next Row (RS): Change to Garter st (knit every row). Work even for 7 rows. BO all sts purlwise.

SLEEVES

Transfer Sleeve sts from st holder to circ needle. With RS facing, rejoin yarn at Sleeve edge, CO 0 (3, 2, 2) sts, knit to end, CO 0 (3, 2, 2) sts–47 (50, 56, 57) sts. Purl 1 row, increase 8 (11, 11, 16) sts evenly across row–55 (61, 67, 73) sts.

Next Row (RS): Change to Lace st. Work even until piece measures 4½ (5, 5½, 6)" [11.5 (12.5, 14, 15) cm] from underarm, ending with a WS row.

Decrease Row (RS): *K1, k2tog; repeat from * to last st, k1–37 (41, 45, 49) sts remain.

Next Row (WS): Change to Garter st. Work even for 12 rows. BO all sts purlwise.

FINISHING

Front and Neck Band: With RS of work facing, pick up and knit 3 sts for every 4 rows along Right Front edge, 1 st for every st across Back neck, and 3 sts for every 4 rows along Left Front edge. Begin Garter st. Work even for 6 rows. BO all sts purlwise.

I-Cord Ties: (make 2) With dpn, CO 2 sts. Work I-Cord as follows: *Transfer needle with sts to left hand, bring yarn around behind work to right-hand side; using second dpn, knit sts from right to left, pulling yarn from left to right for first st; do not turn. Slide sts to opposite end of needle; repeat from * until I-Cord is 6 (6¼, 6½, 6¾)" [15 (16, 16.5, 17) cm] long.

Sew Sleeve and underarm seams. Sew one I-Cord to Right Front edge where Lace st begins. Sew second I-Cord to left underarm. Make two 1" (2.5 cm) Pompoms (see Special Techniques, page 158). Attach Pompoms to ends of I-Cords. Block piece to measurements.

Violet Sacque

THIS LOVELY SACQUE (OR, AS WE MORE COMMONLY SAY TODAY, OPEN CARDIGAN) DEMONSTRATES HOW EASY LACE KNITTING CAN BE. ALTHOUGH THE STITCH PATTERN LOOKS COMPLICATED, IT REQUIRES ONLY ONE TYPE OF INCREASE AND ONE TYPE OF DECREASE AND IS EASY TO MEMORIZE ONCE YOU GET STARTED. THE SWEATER HERE IS SHOWN IN A WONDERFUL FINGERING-WEIGHT ALPACA THAT IS SOFT ENOUGH FOR EVEN THE MOST FINICKY BABY. FOR A COMPLETELY DIFFERENT EFFECT, TRY MAKING IT IN A SMOOTH SOCK YARN. REMEMBER, FOR SAFETY REASONS, GARMENTS WITH RIBBON TIES SHOULD ONLY BE WORN WHEN BABY IS SUPERVISED – IF YOU WISH, LEAVE THEM OFF THE SWEATER AND LET BABY WEAR IT OPEN.

SIZES
6-12 months
(12-18 months, 18-24 months)
Shown in size 6-12 months

FINISHED MEASUREMENTS
20½ (22½, 24½)" [52 (57, 62) cm] chest

YARN
Frog Tree Alpaca Fingering (100% alpaca; 215 yards [197 meters] / 50 grams): 3 skeins #91

NEEDLES
One pair straight needles size US 2 (2.75 mm)
Change needle size if necessary to obtain correct gauge.

NOTIONS
1 yard (1 meter) ⅝" (16 mm) wide grosgrain ribbon

GAUGE
32 sts and 36 rows = 4" (10 cm) in Lace Pattern

NOTE
When working shaping, if you cannot work a complete repeat in Lace Pattern, work remaining sts in St st.

STITCH PATTERN
Lace Pattern (multiple of 8 sts + 1; 12-row repeat) (see Chart)
Rows 1, 3, and 5 (RS): K1, *yo, [k1, k2tog] twice, k1, yo, k1; repeat from * to end.
Row 2 and all WS rows: Purl.
Rows 7, 9, and 11: K1, *k2tog, k1, [yo, k1] twice, k2tog, k1; repeat from * to end.
Row 12: Purl.
Repeat Rows 1-12 for Lace Pattern.

BACK
CO 81 (89, 97) sts. Begin Garter st (knit every row). Work even for 9 rows. Purl 1 row.
Begin Pattern (RS): Change to Lace Pattern (you may follow Chart or text for pattern). Work even until piece measures 6¾ (7½, 8)" [17 (19, 20.5) cm] from the beginning, ending with a WS row.

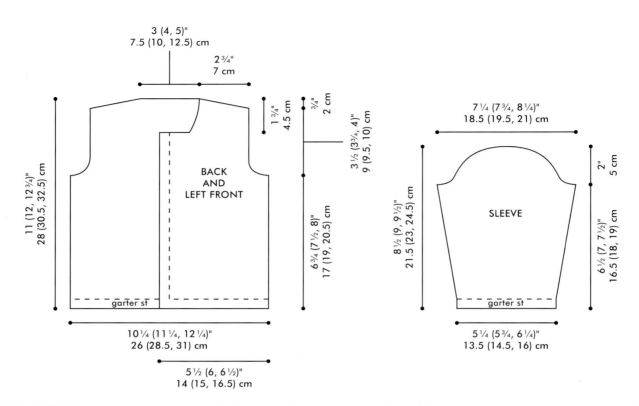

Shape Armholes (RS): BO 4 sts at beginning of next 2 rows, then decrease 1 st each side every other row 4 times–65 (73, 81) sts remain. Work even until piece measures 3½ (3¾, 4)" [9 (9.5, 10) cm] from beginning of shaping, ending with a WS row.

Shape Shoulders (RS): BO 7 sts at beginning of next 6 rows–23 (31, 39) sts remain. BO remaining sts for back neck.

LEFT FRONT

CO 44 (48, 52) sts. Begin Garter st. Work even for 9 rows.

Next Row (WS): K3, purl to end.

Begin Pattern (RS): K0 (4, 0), work in Lace Pattern to last 3 sts, k3.

Work in pattern as established, keeping 3 sts in Garter st at front edge and for size 12-18 months ONLY, keeping 4 sts at seam edge in St st.

Work even until piece measures 6¾ (7½, 8)" [17 (19, 20.5) cm] from the beginning, ending with a WS row.

Shape Armholes (RS): BO 4 sts at armhole edge once, then decrease 1 st at armhole edge every other row 4 times–36 (40, 44) sts remain. Work even until armhole measures 2½ (2¾, 3)" [6.5 (7, 7.5) cm] from beginning of shaping, ending with a RS row.

Shape Neck (WS): BO 12 (16, 20) sts at neck edge once, then decrease 1 st at neck edge every other row 3 times–21 sts remain.

Work even until armhole measures 3½ (3¾, 4)" [9 (9.5, 10) cm] from beginning of shaping, ending with a WS row.

Shape Shoulders: BO 7 sts at armhole edge 3 times.

RIGHT FRONT

Work as for Left Front, reversing shaping and st patterns.

SLEEVES

CO 41 (45, 49) sts. Begin Garter st. Work even for 9 rows. Purl 1 row.

Begin Pattern (RS): K0 (2, 0), work in Lace Pattern to last 0 (2, 0) sts, k0 (2, 0). Work even for 1 row.

Shape Sleeve (RS): Increase 1 st each side this row, then every 6 rows 7 times, working increased sts in Lace Pattern as they become available–57 (61, 65) sts. Work even until piece measures 6½ (7, 7½)" [16.5 (18, 19) cm] from the beginning, ending with a WS row.

Shape Cap (RS): BO 4 sts at beginning of next 2 rows, then 2 st at beginning of next 16 rows–17 (21, 25) sts remain. BO remaining sts.

LACE PATTERN

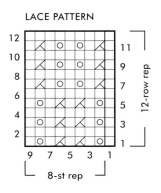

KEY

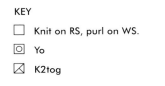

☐ Knit on RS, purl on WS.

⊡ Yo

⊠ K2tog

FINISHING

Block pieces to measurements. Sew shoulder seams.
Collar: With RS facing, beginning at Right
Front, pick up and knit 25 (29, 33) sts along
Right Front neck edge, 23 (31, 39) sts across
Back neck edge, then 25 (29, 33) sts along Left
Front neck edge–73 (89, 105) sts.

Begin Garter st. * Work even for ¾" [2 cm],
ending with a WS row.
Next Row (RS): Knit, increasing 12 (14, 17) sts
evenly spaced across row–85 (103, 122) sts.
Repeat from * once–97 (117, 139) sts.
Work Garter st for ¾" (2 cm). BO all sts loosely.
Set in Sleeves. Sew side and Sleeve seams. Sew
ribbons to WS of Collar, just above pick-up row
(see photo).

Rupert the Lion
&
Elmer the Elephant

RUPERT THE LION IS A SPECIAL TOY THAT DATES TO THE GREAT DEPRESSION,
WHEN PARENTS HAD TO CONSERVE RESOURCES AND CHILDREN HAD FAR FEWER TOYS THAN THEY
DO TODAY. HE MIGHT HAVE BEEN MADE WITH ODDMENTS OF WOOL LEFT OVER FROM
ANOTHER PROJECT OR EVEN FROM YARN RECYCLED FROM AN OLD SWEATER. THE ORIGINAL LOOKED
A LITTLE FEROCIOUS, BUT HERE I'VE GIVEN HIM A SWEET FACE INSTEAD. RUPERT IS STUFFED
WITH ORGANIC COTTON BATTING, BUT YOU CAN USE UNSPUN WOOL ROVING
OR POLYESTER FIBERFILL IF YOU PREFER. BECAUSE HE HAS NO BUTTONS OR HARD PARTS,
HE IS SAFE FOR PLAYING AND HUGGING.

THE ORIGINAL OF THIS 1950S ELEPHANT TOY WAS A STOLID, STURDY GRAY,
BUT I LIKE IT BEST IN PINK – BECAUSE WHO COULDN'T LOVE A PINK ELEPHANT ON PARADE?
LIKE THE OTHER TOYS IN THIS BOOK, ELMER THE ELEPHANT IS CONSTRUCTED FROM
FLAT GARTER-STITCH PIECES THAT ARE SEAMED TOGETHER AND STUFFED. MADE OUT OF CUDDLY,
WASHABLE WOOL AND FILLED WITH SQUEEZABLE COTTON BATTING, HE IS SURE TO
BRING A SMILE TO THE FACE OF ANY BABY.

Rupert the Lion

FINISHED MEASUREMENTS

6 ¼" (16 cm) high at shoulder

YARN

Louet Gems Worsted (100% Merino wool;
175 yards [160 meters] / 100 grams):
1 hank each #05 Goldilocks (MC)
and #02 Ginger (A)
Odd scraps of yarn for embroidering eyes,
nose, and mouth

NEEDLES

One pair straight needles size US 3 (3.25 mm)
One pair double-pointed needles (dpn)
size US 3 (3.25 mm)
Change needle size if necessary to
obtain correct gauge.

NOTIONS

Crochet hook size US L-11 (8 mm);
cotton batting or fiberfill for stuffing;
embroidery needle

GAUGE

22 sts and 30 rows = 4" (10 cm) in
Stockinette st (St st)

NOTES

This pattern is worked at a much tighter
gauge than usually suggested for the yarn to
prevent the stuffing from showing through the
fabric. The body of the Lion is worked in
three pieces. The Left and Right Sides begin
with the hind legs and end with the face of
the Lion. The Underside is worked from the
rear of the Lion to the chest. Four small pieces
are worked to form the Pads of the feet.

LEFT SIDE

With MC, CO 18 sts.
Row 1 (RS): Knit.
Row 2: P1, M1-p, purl to end–19 sts.
Row 3: CO 10 sts, knit to end–29 sts.
Row 4: Repeat Row 2–30 sts.
Rows 5-9: Work in St st.

Shape Foot and Leg

Row 10 (WS): P5, turn; k2tog, k3, turn; p2,
p2tog, turn; k2tog, k1, turn; BO 2 sts. Return
to remaining sts on left-hand needle, BO 7 sts,
purl to end–18 sts remain.
Row 11: Knit.
Row 12: BO 3 sts, purl to end–15 sts remain.
Rows 13-19: Work in St st.
Row 20: P1, M1-p, purl to end–16 sts.
Rows 21-23: Work in St st.
Rows 24-31: Repeat Rows 20-23–18 sts after
Row 28.
Row 32: Purl.
Row 33: K2tog, knit to end–17 sts remain.
Rows 34-47: Work in St st.

Begin Foreleg

Row 48 (WS): CO 13 sts, purl to end–30 sts.
Row 49: Knit to last st, M1, k1–31 sts.
Row 50: Purl.
Row 51: Repeat Row 49–32 sts.
Rows 52-55: Work in St st.

Shape Foot and Leg

Row 56 (WS): P5, turn; k2tog, k3, turn; p2,
p2tog, turn; k2tog, k1, turn; BO 2 sts. Return
to remaining sts on left-hand needle, BO 7 sts,
purl to last st, M1-p, p1–21 sts remain.
Row 57: Knit.

Shape Neck and Head

Row 58 (WS): BO 2 sts, purl to last st, M1-p,
p1–20 sts remain.
Rows 59-62: Repeat Rows 57 and 58–18
sts remain.
Row 63: Knit.
Row 64: Purl to last st, M1-p, p1–19 sts.
Rows 65-71: Work in St st.
Row 72: P2tog, purl to last 2 sts, p2tog–
17 sts remain.
Row 73: Ssk, knit to end–16 sts remain.
Row 74: Purl to last 2 sts, p2tog–15 sts remain.
Row 75: Repeat Row 73–14 sts remain.
Row 76: P2tog, purl to end–13 sts remain.
Row 77: BO 4 sts, knit to end–9 sts remain.
BO all sts.

RIGHT SIDE

With MC, CO 18 sts.
Row 1 (WS): Purl.
Row 2: K1, M1, knit to end–19 sts.
Row 3: CO 10 sts, purl to end–29 sts.
Row 4: Repeat Row 2–30 sts.
Rows 5-9: Work in St st.

Shape Foot and Leg

Row 10 (RS): K5, turn; p2tog, p3, turn; k2,
k2tog, turn; p2tog, p1, turn; BO 2 sts. Return to
remaining sts on left-hand needle, BO 7 sts, knit
to end–18 sts remain.
Row 11: Purl.
Row 12: BO 3 sts, knit to end–15 sts remain.
Rows 13-19: Work in St st.
Row 20: K1, M1, knit to end–16 sts.
Rows 21-23: Work in St st.
Rows 24-31: Repeat Rows 20-23–18 sts
after Row 28.
Row 32: Knit.
Row 33: P2tog, purl to end–17 sts remain.
Rows 34-47: Work in St st.

Begin Foreleg

Row 48 (RS): CO 13 sts, knit to end–30 sts.

Row 49: Purl to last st, M1-p, p1–31 sts.

Row 50: Knit.

Row 51: Repeat Row 49–32 sts.

Rows 52-55: Work in St st.

Shape Foot and Leg

Row 56 (RS): K5, turn; p2tog, p3, turn; k2, k2tog, turn; p2tog, p1, turn; BO 2 sts. Return to remaining sts on left-hand needle, BO 7 sts, knit to last st, M1, k1–21 sts remain.

Row 57: Purl.

Shape Neck and Head

Row 58 (RS): BO 2 sts, knit to last st, M1, k1–20 sts remain.

Rows 59-62: Repeat Rows 57 and 58–18 sts remain.

Row 63: Purl.

Row 64: Knit to last st, M1, k1–19 sts.

Rows 65-71: Work in St st.

Row 72: K2tog, knit to last 2 sts, k2tog–17 sts remain.

Row 73: P2tog, purl to end–16 sts.

Row 74: Knit to last 2 sts, k2tog–15 sts remain.

Row 75: Repeat Row 73–14 sts remain.

Row 76: K2tog, knit to end–13 sts remain.

Row 77: BO 4 sts, purl to end–9 sts remain. BO all sts.

UNDERSIDE

With MC, CO 3 sts.

Row 1 (RS): Knit.

Row 2: P1, M1-p, p1, M1-p, p1–5 sts.

Rows 3-13: Work in St st.

Row 14: CO 16 sts, purl to end–21 sts.

Row 15: CO 16 sts, knit to last st, M1, k1–38 sts.

Row 16: Purl to last st, M1-p, p1–39 sts.

Row 17: Knit to last st, M1, p1–40 sts.

Row 18: Repeat Row 16–41 sts.

Rows 19-21: Work in St st.

Row 22: P5, turn; k2tog, k3, turn; p2, p2tog, turn; k2tog, k1, turn; BO 2 sts. Return to remaining sts on left-hand needle, BO 8 sts, purl to end–28 sts remain.

Row 23: K5, turn; p2tog, p3, turn; k2, k2tog, turn; p2tog, p1, turn; BO 2 sts. Return to remaining sts on left-hand needle, BO 8 sts, knit to end–15 sts remain.

Row 24: BO 3 sts, purl to end–12 sts remain.

Row 25: BO 3 sts, knit to last 2 sts, k2tog–8 sts remain.

Row 26: Purl to last 2 sts, p2tog–7 sts remain.

Rows 27-41: Work in St st.

Row 42: P1, M1-p, purl to last st, M1-p, p1–9 sts.

Row 43: Knit.

Row 44: Repeat Row 42–11 sts.

Rows 45-58: Work in St st.

Row 59: CO 13 sts, knit to end–24 sts

Row 60: CO 13 sts, purl to last st, M1-p, p1–38 sts.

Row 61: Knit to last st, M1, k1–39 sts.

Row 62: Purl to last st, M1-p, p1–40 sts.

Row 63: Repeat Row 61–41 sts.

Rows 64-66: Work in St st.

Row 67: K5, turn; p2tog, p3, turn; k2, k2tog, turn; p2tog, p1, turn; BO 2 sts. Return to remaining sts on left-hand needle, BO 12 sts, knit to end–24 sts remain.

Row 68: P5, turn; k2tog, k3, turn; p2, p2tog, turn; k2tog, k1, turn; BO 2 sts. Return to remaining sts on left-hand needle, BO 12 sts, purl to end–7 sts remain.

Row 69: K2tog, k3, k2tog–5 sts remain.

Rows 70-92: Work in St st.

Row 93: K2tog, k1, k2tog–3 sts remain.

Row 94: Purl. BO all sts.

PADS FOR FEET (make 4)

With MC, CO 3 sts.

Row 1 (RS): Knit.

Row 2: P1, M1-p, p1, M1-p, p1–5 sts.

Rows 3-4: Work in St st.

Row 5: K2tog, k1, k2tog–3 sts remain. BO all sts.

TAIL

Using a crochet hook, attach three 8" (20.5 cm) long strands of yarn to Lion's backside as for Fringe (see Special Techniques, page 158). Holding strands together in pairs, braid strands until tail is 1" (2.5 cm) less than desired length. Tie overhand knot to secure and trim ends even.

Tail Tassel: Cut 4" (10 cm) long strands of A. Thread strands one by one through braid, just above knot, threading strands in different directions. Gather strands below knot, making sure entire knot is hidden. Wrap second piece of yarn tightly around Tassel several times, just below knot; secure ends inside top of Tassel. Trim ends even.

FINISHING

Assemble Body: Block Sides, Underside, and Pads. Sew Left Side and Right Side together from the nose, over the head, and along top of back. Sew Left and Right Sides to Underside, leaving an opening for stuffing. Sew in Pads for Feet. Stuff Lion firmly and sew up opening. Sew Tail into place. With scrap yarn, embroider eyes, nose, and mouth (see photo).

Mane Tuft: Cut 7" (18 cm) long strands of A. Using 2 strands per Fringe, work Fringe around Lion's face, to desired thickness (see photo). Trim ends unevenly.

Elmer the Elephant

FINISHED MEASUREMENTS
7" (18 cm) high

YARN
Louet Gems Worsted Weight (100% Merino wool; 175 yards [160 meters] / 100 grams): 2 hanks # 51 Pink Panther
Odd scraps of yarn for embroidering eyes

NEEDLES
One pair straight needles size US 4 (3.5 mm)
Change needle size if necessary to obtain correct gauge.

NOTIONS
Crochet hook size US F-5 (3.75 mm); stitch holders; fiberfill for stuffing; embroidery needle

GAUGE
22 sts and 32 rows = 4" (10 cm) in Garter stitch (knit every row)

NOTES
This pattern is worked at a much tighter gauge than usually suggested for the yarn to prevent the stuffing from showing through the fabric.

The body of the Elephant is worked in eight pieces. The Body pieces begin with the hind legs and end with the shoulders and neck. The Trunk pieces are worked separately, then joined with the Body. The Underside is worked from the rear of the Elephant to the chest. The Face and Ears are worked last and sewn to the Body as indicated.

BODY (make 2)
CO 29 sts. Begin Garter st (knit every row).
Row 1 (RS): Knit.
Row 2: K1, M1, knit to end—30 sts.
Rows 3-12: Repeat Rows 1 and 2—35 sts after Row 12.
Rows 13-22: Knit.
Row 23: BO 10 sts for rear leg, knit to last st, M1, k1—26 sts remain.
Rows 24-26: Knit.
Row 27: K1, k2tog, knit to last st, M1, k1.
Rows 28-30: Knit.
Rows 31-34: Repeat Rows 27-30.
Row 35: Knit to last st, M1, k1—27 sts.
Rows 36-38: Knit.
Rows 39-42: Repeat Rows 35-38—28 sts.
Row 43: CO 12 sts for front leg, knit to end—40 sts.
Rows 44-64: Knit.
Row 65: BO 15 sts for front leg, knit to end—25 sts remain.
Row 66: Knit.
Row 67: K1, k2tog, knit to end—24 sts remain.
Rows 68-71: Repeat Rows 66 and 67—22 sts remain after Row 71.
Rows 72-74: Knit. Break yarn and transfer 22 sts to st holder.

TRUNK (make 2)
CO 3 sts. Begin Garter st.
Row 1 (RS): K1, M1, k1, M1, k1—5 sts.
Row 2: Knit.
Row 3: K1, M1, knit to last st, M1, k1—7 sts.
Row 4: Knit.
Row 5: K1, M1, knit to last 3 sts, k2tog, k1.
Rows 6 and 7: Repeat Rows 4 and 5.
Row 8: Repeat Row 4.
Row 9: K1, M1, knit to end, CO 5 sts, work across Body sts from st holder—35 sts.
Row 10: Knit.
Row 11: K1, M1, knit to last 3 sts, k2tog, k1.
Rows 12-14: Knit.
Row 15: K1, k2tog, knit to last 3 sts, k2tog, k1—33 sts remain.
Row 16: Knit.

Rows 17-20: Repeat Rows 15 and 16—29 sts remain after Row 19.
Row 21: Repeat Row 15—27 sts remain.
Row 22: BO 5 sts, knit to end—22 sts remain.
Row 23: K1, k2tog, knit to last 3 sts, k2tog, k1—20 sts remain.
Rows 24-27: Repeat Rows 22 and 23—6 sts remain after row 27. BO all sts.

UNDERSIDE
CO 38 sts. Begin Garter st.
Row 1 (RS): Knit.
Rows 2-21: Knit.
Rows 22 and 23: BO 10 sts at beginning of row—18 sts remain after Row 23.
Rows 24-26: Knit.
Row 27: K1, k2tog, knit to last 3 sts, k2tog, k1—16 sts remain.
Rows 28-30: Knit.
Row 31: Repeat Row 27—14 sts remain.
Rows 32-39: Knit.
Rows 40 and 41: CO 12 sts at beginning of row—38 sts after Row 41.
Rows 42-63: Knit. BO all sts.

FACE
CO 2 sts. Begin Garter st.
Row 1 (RS): K1, M1, k1—3 sts.
Row 2: Knit.
Row 3: K1, M1, k1, M1, k1—5 sts.
Row 4: Knit.
Row 5: K1, M1, knit to last st, M1, k1—7 sts.
Rows 6-8: Knit.
Rows 9-24: Repeat Rows 5-8—15 sts after Row 21. Work even until piece measures 5½" (14 cm) from the beginning, ending with a WS row.
Row 1 (RS): K1, k2tog, knit to last 3 sts, k2tog, k1—13 sts remain.
Rows 2 and 3: Knit.
Rows 4-18: Repeat Rows 1-3—3 sts remain after Row 16.
Row 19: K3tog—1 st remains. Fasten off.

EARS (make 2)

CO 3 sts. Begin Garter st.

Row 1 (RS): K1, M1, k1, M1, k1–5 sts.

Row 2: Knit.

Row 3: K1, M1, knit to last st, M1, k1–7 sts.

Rows 4-9: Repeat Rows 2 and 3–13 sts after Row 9.

Rows 10-12: Knit.

Row 13: K1, M1, knit to last st, M1, k1–15 sts.

Rows 14-17: Repeat Rows 10-13–17 sts.

Work even until piece measures 3" (7.5 cm) from the beginning, ending with a WS row.

Row 1 (RS): BO 3 sts, knit to end–14 sts remain.

Row 2: Knit to last 3 sts, k2tog, k1–13 sts remain.

Row 3: K1, k2tog, knit to end–12 sts remain.

Rows 4-8: Knit.

Row 9: K1, k2tog, knit to last 3 sts, k2tog, k1–10 sts remain.

Row 10: Knit.

Rows 11-14: Repeat Rows 9 and 10–6 sts remain after Row 13. BO all sts.

FINISHING

Block pieces lightly. Sew Underside to legs and tummy of Elephant. Sew Body pieces together along back, up to where Trunk was joined to Body sts. Insert Face in between Trunk pieces at top of back and sew to Trunk pieces, leaving opening at top of head for stuffing, and ending at end of Trunk BO edge. Sew Trunk edges together. Stuff Elephant firmly and sew closed. Sew Ears in position (see photo). With scrap yarn, embroider eyes (see photo).

TAIL

Attach six 8" (20.5 cm) long strands of yarn to Elephant's backside as for Fringe (see Special Techniques, page 158). Holding strands together in pairs, braid strands until tail is 1" (2.5 cm) less than desired length. Tie overhand knot to secure and trim ends even.

Bunny Blanket

THE 1946 ORIGINAL OF THIS APPLIQUÉD BLANKET WAS WORKED IN PLAIN STOCKINETTE STITCH,
BUT I CHOSE AN EASY DAISY STITCH INSTEAD TO MAKE THE PROCESS OF KNITTING THE BLANKET MORE INTERESTING.
THE GRASSLIKE TEXTURE OF THE STITCH PATTERN ALSO GIVES THE FABRIC BUNNIES AN APPROPRIATE
BACKGROUND ON WHICH TO CAVORT. BE SURE TO PRESHRINK THE FABRIC YOU USE FOR THE BUNNIES (BY PREWASHING
AND DRYING IT), SO THEY DON'T CAUSE THE FINISHED BLANKET TO PUCKER WHEN YOU LAUNDER IT.

FINISHED MEASUREMENTS
33" wide x 44" long (84 cm x 112 cm)

YARN
Sheep Shop Yarn Company Sheep 3
(70% wool / 30% silk; 325 yards [297
meters] / 100 grams): 4 hanks #F31

NEEDLES
One 32" (80 cm) circular (circ) needle
size US 5 (3.75 mm)
Change needle size if necessary
to obtain correct gauge.

NOTIONS
Crochet hook size F-5 (3.75 mm);
¼ yard [.25 meters] cotton quilting fabric
or cotton flannel, for appliqué;
embroidery thread for appliqué;
embroidery needle

GAUGE
20 sts and 24 rows = 4" (10 cm)
in Daisy Pattern

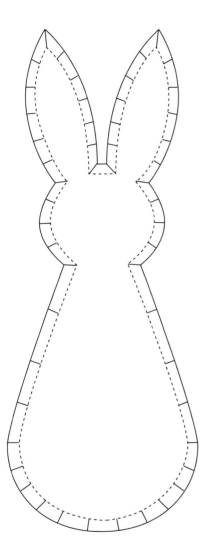

ABBREVIATION

DS (Daisy Stitch): P3tog, but do not drop sts from left-hand needle, wrap yarn around right-hand needle, p3tog these same 3 sts, drop sts from left-hand needle together.

STITCH PATTERN

Daisy Pattern (multiple of 4 sts + 1; 4-row repeat)
Rows 1 and 3 (RS): Knit.
Row 2: K1, *DS, k1; repeat from * to end.
Row 4: K1, p1, k1, *DS, k1; repeat from * to end of row, end p1, k1.
Repeat Rows 1-4 for Daisy Pattern.

BLANKET

CO 165 sts. Begin Daisy Pattern. Work even until piece measures 44" (112 cm) from the beginning, ending with a WS row. BO all sts.

FINISHING

Block lightly. Using crochet hook, work 1 rnd single crochet evenly around entire Blanket, join with Slip st to first st. Fasten off.

Appliqué Bunnies

Before beginning, wash and dry fabric on hottest settings to preshrink it.

To create bunny templates, trace or copy bunny illustration, shrinking or enlarging it to desired size. *Note: Large bunny shown is 7½" high x 3¼" wide (19 x 8.5 cm) (at widest point). Small bunny is 6" high x 2¾" wide (15 x 7 cm) (approximately 80% of size of large bunny).* Pin template to fabric.

Make 2 large bunnies and 4 small bunnies. Cut bunnies along outer edge of template; cut notches in outer edge where indicated. Fold fabric to WS at dotted line, making additional notches if necessary so that fabric lies flat. Press bunnies flat.

Pin bunnies in place (see photo). Attach bunnies to Blanket using embroidery thread and Blanket stitch as follows: Thread embroidery needle with embroidery thread. Working from left to right, along bottom edge of bunny, bring thread up from WS, just outside edge of bunny. Insert needle from RS to WS, at a point ¼" (6 mm) in from edge of bunny and ¼" (6 mm) to left of first hole, then bring needle from WS to RS, in straight line down from last hole, and just outside edge of bunny, with tip of needle in front of thread, so that it forms a "corner." *Bring needle from RS to WS to RS again, holding tip of needle in front of thread. Repeat from * around entire edge of bunny.

Horace the Horse

HORACE IS KNITTED FLAT IN PIECES, THEN SEAMED AND STUFFED.
FROM A 1939 BOOK IN THE FASHIONABLE MINERVA PATTERN LINE, HE DEMONSTRATES THE
WONDERFUL SENSE OF STYLIZATION THAT WAS TYPICAL OF THE 1930S. I CAN'T LOOK AT HORACE
WITHOUT BEING REMINDED OF THE ART DECO TOYS FROM THE 1934 FILM *BABES IN TOYLAND.*

FINISHED MEASUREMENTS
11" (28 cm) high

YARN
Mission Falls 1824 Wool (100% superwash Merino wool; 85 yards [78 meters] / 50 grams): 4 skeins #001 Natural (MC); 2 skeins #008 Earth (A); 1 skein each #005 Raven (B) and #011 Poppy (C)

NEEDLES
One pair straight needles size US 5 (3.75 mm)
Change needle size if necessary to obtain correct gauge.

NOTIONS
Crochet hook size US F-5 (3.75 mm); stitch holders; fiberfill for stuffing; tapestry needle; embroidery needle

GAUGE
19 sts and 36 rows = 4" (10 cm) in Garter st (knit every row)

NOTES
This pattern is worked at a much tighter gauge than usually suggested for the yarn to prevent the stuffing from showing through the fabric. The body of the Horse is worked in five main pieces. The Right and Left Sides are exactly the same. They begin with the rear end and legs and end at the Head and front legs. The Middle Section begins at the chest, works over the head and neck, across the back and rear end, to the underside of the Horse, splitting to form the front and back of each leg. The Inside of Legs section forms the last portion of each leg.

RIGHT AND LEFT SIDES (both alike)
Back
With MC, CO 8 sts.
Row 1 (RS): K1, M1, knit to end–9 sts.
Rows 2 and 3: Repeat Row 1–11 sts.
Row 4: Knit.
Row 5: Repeat Row 1–12 sts.
Row 6: Knit.
Rows 7-9: Repeat Row 1–15 sts after Row 9.
Row 10: Knit.

Row 11: K1, M1, knit to last st, M1, k1–17 sts.
Row 12: Knit to end, CO 20 sts–37 sts.
Row 13: K1, M1, k20, M1, knit to end–39 sts.
Row 14: Repeat Row 1–40 sts.
Row 15: Knit.
Row 16: Knit to last st, M1, k1–41 sts.
Rows 17-24: Repeat Rows 15 and 16–45 sts after Row 24.
Row 25: BO 25 sts, knit to last 3 sts, k2tog, k1–19 sts remain.
Rows 26-32: Knit.
Row 33: Knit to last 3 sts, k2tog, k1–18 sts remain.
Rows 34-40: Knit.
Row 41: Repeat Row 33–17 sts remain.
Rows 42-47: Knit.
Break yarn, place sts on holder for Back, and set aside.

Neck and Front Leg
With MC, CO 8 sts.
Row 1 (WS): K1, M1, knit to last st, M1, k1–10 sts.
Rows 2-6: Repeat Row 1–20 sts after Row 6.
Row 7: Knit to end, CO 1 st, work across Back sts from holder, with WS of Back sts facing, CO 25 sts–63 sts.

Front Body
Row 1 (RS): Continuing with sts from Back and Neck, knit.
Row 2: K1, M1, knit to end–64 sts.
Row 3: K1, k2tog, knit to end–63 sts remain.
Row 4: Knit.
Row 5: K1, k2tog, knit to last st, M1, k1.
Row 6: Knit.
Row 7: Repeat Row 3–62 sts remain.
Row 8: Repeat Row 2–63 sts.
Row 9: Repeat Row 3–62 sts remain.

Row 10: Knit.
Row 11: BO 20 sts, k17, place last 24 sts on holder for Head–18 sts remain.
Row 12: K1, k2tog, knit to last 3 sts, k2tog, k1–16 sts remain.
Rows 13-17: Repeat Row 12–6 sts remain after Row 17.
BO all sts.

Head
With RS facing, rejoin yarn to sts on holder for Head.
Row 1 (RS): BO 4 sts, knit to end–20 sts remain.
Rows 2 and 3: K1, M1, knit to end–22 sts after Row 3.
Row 4: Knit to last st, M1, k1–23 sts.
Rows 5 and 6: Repeat Rows 3 and 4–25 sts after Row 6.
Row 7: Repeat Row 2–26 sts.
Rows 8-13: Knit.
Row 14: K1, k2tog, knit to end–25 sts remain.
Row 15: Knit.
Row 16: Repeat Row 14–24 sts remain.
Row 17: Knit.
Rows 18 and 19: Repeat Row 14–22 sts remain after Row 19.
Row 20: K1, k2tog, knit to last 3 sts, k2tog, k1–20 sts remain.
Row 21: BO 5 sts, knit to end–15 sts remain.
Row 22: Repeat Row 14–14 sts remain.
Row 23: BO 2 sts, knit to end–12 sts remain.
Row 24: Repeat Row 14–11 sts remain.
Row 25: Knit.
Row 26: Repeat Row 20–9 sts remain.
Row 27: Knit to last 3 sts, k2tog, k1–8 sts remain.
BO all sts.

MIDDLE SECTION
With MC, CO 16 sts. Begin Garter st (knit every row). Work even until piece measures 26" (66 cm) from the beginning.
Divide for Legs: Work 8 sts, join a second ball of yarn, work to end. Working both sides at the same time, work even until piece measures 8½" (21.5 cm) from beginning of Legs.
Join Legs: Work across all sts; break second ball of yarn–16 sts. Work even until piece measures 2½" (6.5 cm) from join. Repeat from * to *. BO all sts.

INSIDE OF LEGS (make 2)
With MC, CO 44 sts.
Row 1 and all WS rows: Knit.
Row 2: K21, k2tog, knit to end–43 sts remain.
Rows 4 and 6: K20, k2tog, knit to end–41 sts remain after Row 6.
Rows 8 and 10: K19, k2tog, knit to end–39 sts remain after Row 10.
Row 12: K18, k2tog, knit to end–38 sts remain.
BO all sts.

FINISHING
Beginning at chest, working over head, neck, back, rear and hind legs, and ending with front legs, sew Middle Section to each Side, leaving opening at top of neck for stuffing. Sew Insides of Legs to Middle Section. Stuff Horse with fiberfill and sew opening closed.

Embroidery: Using embroidery needle and 2 strands of B held together, work Sideways Duplicate st around face for halter (see photo) as follows:
Note: This st differs from standard Duplicate st in that you are not working up and down within a stitch, but are rather working across the st from side to side.

Begin by using a single strand of yarn to trace the baseline you want you the duplicate st to take around the face or belly, loosely anchoring the strand by running it through a single st at the beginning and end of the line. With tapestry needle and 2 strands of yarn held together, holding piece so that baseline is vertical, bring needle through bottom side of first st to be covered, then thread needle from right to left behind vertical bar between this st and the next st directly above it. Take needle back through both sides of st just covered, working from bottom to top, and making sure not to pull st too tightly. *Skip the next st vertically, thread needle from right to left behind vertical bar between skipped st and the next st directly above it. Take needle back through both sides of st just covered. Repeat from * to desired end point, making sure to keep tension even. You may leave the baseline in place and work over it, or remove it as you work. Work a second line of Sideways Duplicate st next to the first line.

Using embroidery needle and 2 strands of C held together, work Sideways Duplicate st around belly for harness. Embroider eyes (see photo).

Halter Tassels (make 2): Using C, wrap yarn approximately 20 times (or to desired thickness) around palm of hand. Cut end of yarn. Slide wrapped yarn off hand and tie single strand of yarn tightly around center of wrapped strands. Attach Tassels to sides of halter at center tie; separate loops to hide tie.

Tail Tassel: Make Tassel as for halter, wrapping yarn approximately 60 times. Attach to rear end.

Mane: Cut 7" (18 cm) long strands of A. Using 2 strands per Fringe, work Fringe (see Special Techniques, page 158) along back of Horse's neck, to desired thickness (see photo). Trim ends unevenly.

knitting in the 1930s

During the Depression, knitting's popularity soared to new heights. Approximately 10 million Americans—more than one-twelfth of the population—knit in the 1930s. Yarn companies published thousands of patterns, trained instructors for department stores, and devised hundreds of new and exciting yarns. Knitters purchased 10 million pairs of knitting needles in 1934. Knitting contests drew tens of thousands of participants nationwide. Even First Ladies knitted, including Grace Coolidge, Lou Henry Hoover, and Eleanor Roosevelt, as did glamorous movie stars like Ginger Rogers and Joan Blondell. The knitting craze extended to Paris as well, where top fashion designers like Schiaparelli, Lanvin, and Vionnet produced the latest in knit styles—which would be copied by hand-knitters around the world. As Susan Strawn wrote in *Knitting America,*" hand-knitting proved one of the few Depression-resistant industries during the 1930s."

And why not? Knitting was not just fun but useful and economical. After the stock market crash of 1929, yarn prices went down. It became a "fashionable virtue" to knit your own garments rather than buy them ready-made. People had little money for entertainment, let alone clothes—and hand-knitting satisfied the need for both.

Yet knitting was a more difficult proposition in the 1930s than it is today. Patterns came without charts, and indeed without detailed instructions; knitters were expected to know how to perform every technique without much help from the pattern. And knitting was not for the faint of heart. Striving to make long-lasting garments that would stand up to hard wear, knitters of the 1930s steeled themselves to make the long, drapey garments fashionable at the time at an average gauge of 7 to 9 stitches per inch. An adult skirt might require casting on 600 stitches at a time.

Baby garments, then, were the perfect option for those knitters with short attention spans. A baby garment took just a fraction of the time to make, and allowed knitters to practice the skills they would later use on adult-sized garments.

At the end of the decade, Europe was again plunged into war and millions were ready to heed the call for charity knits—which would serve them well during the tumultuous years to come.

Dewey Cabled Pullover

THIS BOATNECK PULLOVER, OR "SLIPOVER" AS IT WAS ORIGINALLY CALLED, FEATURES AN
EXTREMELY SIMPLE DROP-SHOULDER CONSTRUCTION PAIRED WITH AN EASY CABLE WITH ONLY ONE TWIST
THAT ALWAYS GOES IN THE SAME DIRECTION. IT IS WORKED IN ONE PIECE, WITH THE DESIRED NUMBER
OF STITCHES BOUND OFF AT THE NECK AND THEN CAST ON AGAIN AFTER THE SHOULDERS ARE WORKED. I SELECTED
A SOFT, MACHINE-WASHABLE PURE MERINO WOOL COMMONLY USED FOR SOCK YARN FOR THIS PULLOVER
BECAUSE I WANTED TO ENSURE THAT IT WAS SMOOTH-SURFACED AND STURDY.

SIZES
9-12 months
(12-18 months, 18-24 months)
Shown in size 9-12 months

FINISHED MEASUREMENTS
19 ½ (21 ½, 23 ½)"
[50 (55, 60) cm] chest

YARN
Artyarns Ultramerino 4 (100% Merino
wool; 191 yards [175 meters] / 50 grams):
3 (3, 4) hanks #260

NEEDLES
One pair straight needles size US 3
(3.25 mm)
Change needle size if necessary to
obtain correct gauge.

GAUGE
32 sts and 40 rows = 4" (10 cm)
in Stockinette stitch (St st)

NOTE
The Body is worked in one piece from
bottom edge of Back, over the shoulders,
to bottom edge of Front.

ABBREVIATIONS
T1R: K3tog, but do not drop sts from left-hand
needle, slip first of these 3 sts to right-hand
needle, knit second of these sts, slipping second
and third sts from left-hand needle together.

STITCH PATTERNS
1x1 Rib (multiple of 2 sts; 1-row repeat)
Row 1 (RS): *K1, p1; repeat from * to end
[end k1 if an odd number of sts].
Row 2: Knit the knit sts and purl the purl sts
as they face you. Repeat Row 2 for 1x1 Rib.

**Cable Panel (panel of 15 sts after Set-Up Row;
8-row repeat)**
Set-Up Row (RS): P3, [M1, k1, M1, p3] twice—15 sts.
Rows 1, 3, 5, and 7: K3, [p3, k3] twice.
Row 2: P3, [T1R, p3] twice.
Rows 4, 6, and 8: P3 [k3, p3] twice.
Repeat Rows 1-8 for Cable Panel.

BODY

Back

CO 76 (84, 92) sts. Begin 1x1 Rib. *Work even for 1½" (4 cm), ending with a WS row.

Establish Cable Pattern (RS): Work in St st over 18 (21, 24) sts, work Cable Panel over next 11 sts, working increases as indicated, work in St st over 18 (20, 22) sts, work Cable Panel over next 11 sts, working increases as indicated, work in St st over 18 (21, 24) sts–84 (92, 100) sts. * Work even until piece measures approximately 10 ¼ (11, 12)" [26 (28, 30.5) cm] from the beginning, ending with Row 2 of Cable Panel.

Decrease Row (RS): K18 (21, 24), p3, [k3tog, p3] twice, p18 (20, 22), p3, [k3tog, p3] twice, p18 (21, 24)–76 (84, 92) sts remain.

Next Row (RS): Change to 1x1 Rib. Work even for 1½"(4 cm), ending with a WS row.

Shape Neck (RS) and Shoulders: Work 14 (17, 20) sts, join a second ball of yarn, BO 48 (50, 52) sts, work to end–14 (17, 20) sts remain for each shoulder. Working both sides at same time, work even for 1" (2.5 cm), ending with a WS row. Break yarn on left shoulder.

Front

Next Row (RS): Continuing in 1x1 Rib, work to neck opening, CO 48 (50, 52) sts for Front neck, work to end–76 (84, 92) sts. Work as for Back from * to *. Work even until piece measures 10½ (11, 12)" [26 (28, 30.5) cm] from sts CO for neck, ending with Row 1 of Cable Panel. Work Decrease Row as for Back–76 (84, 92) sts remain.

Next Row (RS): Change to 1x1 Rib. Work even for 1½" [4 cm], ending with a WS row. BO all sts in pattern.

SLEEVES

CO 46 sts. Begin 1x1 Rib. Work even for 1½" (4 cm), ending with a WS row.

Next Row (RS): Change to St st. Work even for 8 rows.

Shape Sleeve (RS): Increase 1 st each side this row, then every 6 (6, 4) rows 6 (8, 10) times, as follows: K1, M1, knit to last st, M1, k1–60 (64, 68) sts. Work even until piece measures 7 (7½, 8)" [18 (19, 20.5) cm] from the beginning, ending with a WS row. BO all sts.

FINISHING

Block pieces to measurements. Fold Body in half lengthwise. Place markers 3¾ (4, 4¼)" [9.5 (10, 11) cm] down from shoulder on either side. Sew in Sleeves between markers. Sew side and Sleeve seams.

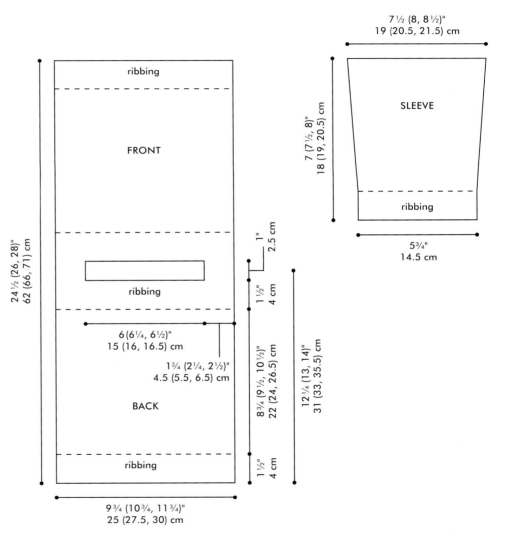

Cleo Kitty Slippers

EASY AND QUICK TO MAKE, THESE LITTLE SLIPPERS ARE KNITTED BACK AND FORTH
ON TWO NEEDLES, THEN SEWN INTO DARLING LITTLE MARY JANES WITH WEE KITTEN EARS. THESE WILL TURN
OUT EQUALLY WELL IN WOOL OR COTTON; IF YOUR LITTLE ONE IS WALKING, BE SURE TO USE
SOMETHING TIGHTLY SPUN FOR DURABILITY AND MAKE SURE SHE STAYS ON NON-SLIPPERY SURFACES. A PAIR
ONLY REQUIRES 125 TO 150 YARDS OF YARN AND CAN BE WHIPPED UP IN AN EVENING OR TWO.

SIZES
6-12 (12-24) months
Shown in size 12-24 months

FINISHED MEASUREMENTS
4½ (5)" [11.5 (12.5) cm] long

YARN
Rowan Yarns 4-Ply Cotton (100% cotton;
186 yards [170 meters] / 50 grams):
1 ball #133 Cheeky
Odd scraps of yarn for embroidering eyes,
whiskers, and nose

NEEDLES
One pair straight needles size US 2 (2.75 mm)
Change needle size if necessary to obtain
correct gauge.

NOTIONS
Two ³⁄₈" (10 mm) buttons; embroidery needle

GAUGE
14 sts and 28 rows = 2" (5 cm) in Garter st
(Knit every row)

NOTES
The Slipper is cast on at one side of the sole,
and is then worked across the sole, up one
side of the "Upper", across the front, and
down the opposite side of the "Upper". The
bound-off edge of the second side is then
sewn to the cast-on edge of the sole, and
the two sides of the heel are sewn together.

SLIPPER
SOLE
CO 21 (24) sts. Begin Garter st (knit every row).
Work even for 1 row.

Shape Sole

Increase Row (RS): Increase 1 st each side this row, then every other row 3 (4) times, as follows: K1, M1, knit to last st, M1, k1–29 (34) sts. Work even for 1 row.

Decrease Row (RS): Decrease 1 st each side this row, then every other row 3 (4) times, as follows: K1, ssk, knit to last 3 sts, k2tog, k1–21 (24) sts remain.

UPPER

Shape First Side of Upper (WS): Using Cable CO (see Special Techniques, page 158), CO 6 (7) sts, knit across CO sts, work to last st, M1, k1–28 (32) sts. Work even for 1 row.

Increase Row (WS): Increase 1 st at end of this row, then every other row 4 (5) times, as follows: Knit to last st, M1, k1–33 (38) sts. Work even for 1 row.

Shape Top of Upper (WS): BO 19 (23) sts, work to end–14 (15) sts remain. Work even for 13 (15) rows.

Shape Second Side of Upper (WS): Using Cable CO, CO 19 (23) sts, knit across CO sts, work to last 3 sts, k2tog, k1–32 (37) sts. Work even for 1 row.

Decrease Row (WS): Decrease 1 st at end of this row, then every other row 4 (5) times, as follows: Knit to last 3 sts, k2tog, k1–27 (31) sts remain. BO all sts.

EARS (make 4)

CO 9 sts. Begin Garter st. Work even for 6 rows.

Shape Ears

Row 1: K3, k3tog, k3–7 sts remain. Work even for 1 row.
Row 3: K2, k3tog, k2–5 sts remain. Work even for 1 row.
Row 5: K1, k3tog, k1–3 sts remain. BO all sts.

FINISHING

Sew CO edge of Sole to BO edge of second side of Upper. Sew back of heel together, then sew base of heel to Sole. Sew toe to Sole, easing excess fabric at toe. Sew Ears to front (see photo).

ANKLE STRAPS (make 2)

Place marker 6 (7) sts to either side of heel seam. Using Cable CO, CO 12 (13) sts, knit across CO sts, pick up and knit 12 (14) sts between markers, turn, using Cable CO, CO 12 (13) sts, knit across CO sts, knit 14 sts to end–36 (40) sts. Begin Garter st. Work even for 4 rows.

BO all sts. Sew button to one end of Strap (sew to opposite end on each Slipper). Using crochet hook, work crochet chain (see Special Techniques, page 158) long enough to fit snugly around button. Sew to Strap opposite button.

Using scrap yarn, embroider eyes, nose, and whiskers (see photo).

Felix Cardigan & Pants Set

THIS SHORT PANTS AND CARDIGAN SET WAS TYPICAL BABY FASHION IN THE 1950S.
THE KITTY CATS THAT ADORN THE CARDIGAN ARE AN EASY INTRODUCTION TO
STRANDED KNITTING. THE SHORT PANTS ARE DARLING ON ANY BABY, BUT IF YOU PREFER "LONGIES,"
SIMPLY BUY EXTRA YARN AND WORK THE LEGS TO YOUR DESIRED LENGTH.

SIZES

3-6 months
(6-12 months, 12-18 months)
Shown in size 6-12 months

FINISHED MEASUREMENTS

CARDIGAN: 20½ (21½, 23)"
[52 (55, 58) cm] chest, buttoned
PANTS: 18 (20, 22)"
[46 (51, 56) cm] waist

YARN

Cherry Tree Hill Yarn Supersock Solids
(100% superwash Merino wool;
420 yards [384 meters] / 100 grams):
CARDIGAN: 2 (2, 3) hanks Natural (MC);
1 (1, 1) hank Mint (A); PANTS: Small
amount of MC; 2 (2, 3) hanks Mint (A)

NEEDLES

One pair straight needles
size US 2 (2.75 mm)
One pair straight needles
size US 3 (3.25 mm)
Change needle size if necessary
to obtain correct gauge.

NOTIONS

CARDIGAN: Stitch holders; six ⅝" (16 mm)
buttons; ¾ yard (.75 meter) 1" (2.5 cm)
wide grosgrain ribbon; sewing needle
and thread
PANTS: Stitch holders; stitch markers; ¾
yard (.75 meter) 1" (2.5 cm) wide elastic;
sewing needle and thread

GAUGE

28 sts and 40 rows = 4" (10 cm) in Stockinette stitch (St st), using larger needles

NOTE

Armhole shaping and Charts are worked
simultaneously. Please read entire section
through before beginning.

STITCH PATTERN

2x2 Rib (multiple of 4 sts + 2; 1-row repeat)
Row 1 (RS): K2, *p2, k2; repeat from * to end.
Row 2: Knit the knit sts and purl the purl sts as
they face you. Repeat Row 2 for 2x2 Rib.

CARDIGAN

BACK
Using smaller needles and MC, CO 70 (74, 78)
sts. Begin 2x2 Rib. Work even for 1" (2.5 cm),
ending with a WS row.
(RS) Change to larger needles and St st, beginning
with a knit row, increase 2 sts evenly spaced on
first row—72 (76, 80) sts. Work even until piece
measures 6½ (7½, 8½)" [16.5 (19, 21.5) cm]
from the beginning, ending with a WS row.

Shape Armholes (RS): BO 3 sts at beginning of next 2 rows, then decrease 1 st each side every other row twice–62 (66, 70) sts remain. Work even until armholes measure 3¾ (4, 4¼)" [9.5 (10, 11) cm] from beginning of shaping, ending with a WS row.

Shape Shoulders and Neck (RS): BO 19 (21, 22) sts at beginning of next 2 rows–24 (24, 26) sts remain. BO all sts.

RIGHT FRONT

Using smaller needles and A, CO 40 (43, 46) sts.

Begin Pattern (RS): K6 (7, 8) (Button Band sts, keep in St st), work in 2x2 Rib to end, beginning with p2. Work even for 1" (2.5 cm), ending with a WS row.

Next Row (RS): Change to larger needles and St st. Work even until piece measures 5 (6, 7)" [12.5 (15, 18) cm] from the beginning, ending with a WS row.

Begin Fair Isle Pattern (RS): Work Fair Isle pattern from Chart A. Work even until Chart A is complete.

Next Row (RS): Change to MC. Work even for 2 rows.

Note: Armhole shaping and Chart are worked simultaneously. Please read entire section through before beginning.

Next Row (RS): Work 7 (9, 11) sts, work Fair Isle pattern from Chart B across next 26 sts, work to end. Work even until Chart B is complete.

Next Row (WS): Change to MC. Work even for 2 rows.

Next Row (WS): Work across Chart A, aligning pattern with previous repeat of Chart. *Note: Work odd-numbered rows as WS rows and even-numbered rows as RS rows. You will not have a complete repeat at armhole edge.* Work even until Chart is complete. Change to MC.

AT THE SAME TIME, when piece measures same as for Back to armhole, shape armhole as for Back–35 (38, 41) sts remain. Work even until armhole measures 2¾ (3, 3¼)" [7 (7.5, 8.5) cm] from beginning of shaping, ending with a RS row.

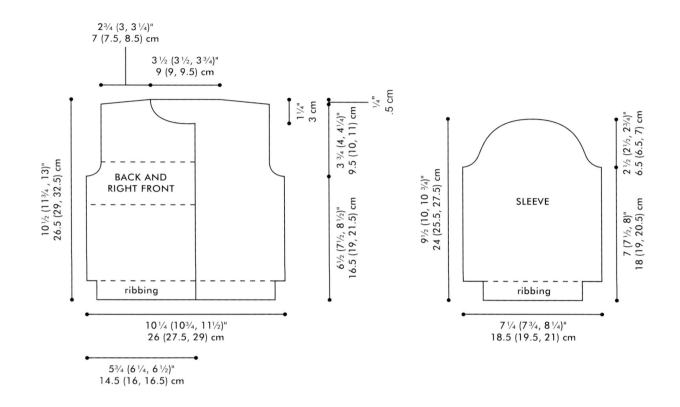

2¾ (3, 3¼)"
7 (7.5, 8.5) cm

3½ (3½, 3¾)"
9 (9, 9.5) cm

BACK AND
RIGHT FRONT

ribbing

10½ (11¾, 13)"
26.5 (29, 32.5) cm

10¼ (10¾, 11½)"
26 (27.5, 29) cm

5¾ (6¼, 6½)"
14.5 (16, 16.5) cm

1¼"
3 cm

3¾ (4, 4¼)"
9.5 (10, 11) cm

¼"
.5 cm

6½ (7½, 8½)"
16.5 (19, 21.5) cm

SLEEVE

ribbing

9½ (10, 10¾)"
24 (25.5, 27.5) cm

7¼ (7¾, 8¼)"
18.5 (19.5, 21) cm

2½ (2½, 2¾)"
6.5 (6.5, 7) cm

7 (7½, 8)"
18 (19, 20.5) cm

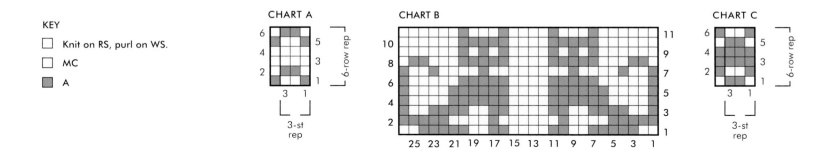

KEY

☐ Knit on RS, purl on WS.

☐ MC

▨ A

CHART A

6-row rep

3-st rep

CHART B

CHART C

6-row rep

3-st rep

Shape Neck (WS): Work 10 (11, 13) sts and place on holder for Neckband, work to end.

Next Row (RS): Decrease 1 st at neck edge this row, then every other row 5 times—19 (21, 22) sts remain. Work even until armhole measures same as for Back to shoulder shaping, shape shoulder as for Back. Place markers for five buttons along Front edge, the first ½" (1.5 cm) from bottom, and the remaining 4 approximately every 1¾ (2, 2¼)" [4.5 (5, 5.5) cm] apart. *Note: The sixth button will be placed in the Neckband once the cardigan is completed, ½" (1.5 cm) above the beginning of Front neck shaping. Adjust the spacing of markers if necessary to accommodate this last button.*

LEFT FRONT

Using smaller needles and A, CO 40 (43, 46) sts.
Begin Pattern (RS): Work in 2x2 Rib to last 6 (7, 8) sts, k6 (7, 8) (Buttonhole Band sts, keep in St st). Work even for ½" (1.5 cm), ending with a RS row.
Buttonhole Row (WS): P2 (3, 3), BO 2 sts, work to end. Work even for 1 row, CO 2 sts over BO sts. Work even until piece measures 1" (2.5 cm) from the beginning, ending with a WS row. **(RS)** Change to larger needles and St st. Complete as for Right Front, working buttonholes opposite markers and reversing shaping and st patterns.

SLEEVES

Using smaller needles and MC, CO 42 (46, 50) sts. Begin 2x2 Rib. Work even for 1" (2.5 cm).
Next Row (RS): Change to larger needles and St st, increase 9 (8, 7) sts evenly across row—51 (54, 57) sts. Work even for 1 row.
Begin Fair Isle Pattern (RS): Work Fair Isle pattern from Chart A. Work even until Chart A is complete.
Next Row (RS): Change to MC. Work even until piece measures 7 (7½, 8)" [18 (19, 20.5) cm] from the beginning, ending with a WS row.
Shape Cap (RS): BO 2 sts at beginning of next 2 rows, decrease 1 st each side every other row 8 (9,

10) times, then every row 6 times—19 (20, 21) sts remain. BO all sts.

FINISHING

Block pieces to measurements. Sew shoulder seams. Set in Sleeves. Sew side and Sleeve seams.
Neckband: With RS facing, using smaller needles and MC, work across sts from holder for Right Front, pick up and knit 13 sts along Right Front neck edge, 24 (24, 26) sts across Back neck, 13 sts along Left Front neck edge, then work across sts from holder for Left Front—70 (72, 78) sts.
Begin Pattern (WS): P6 (7, 8) (edge sts, keep in St st), work in 2x2 Rib, beginning with k2, to last 6 (7, 8) sts, p6 (7, 8) (edge sts, keep in St st). Work even until piece measures ½" (1.5 cm) from pick-up row, ending with a RS row. Work buttonhole as for Left Front. Work even for ¾" (2 cm). BO all sts in pattern.
Sew ribbon to WS of Front bands; cut slits for buttonholes and sew edges of slits to prevent fraying. Sew buttons opposite buttonholes.

PANTS

FRONT

Legs (make 2)
Using larger needles and A, CO 37 (40, 43) sts. Begin St st. Work even for 5 rows. Knit 1 row (turning row). Work in St st for 6 rows, beginning with a knit row.
Begin Fair Isle Pattern (RS): Work Fair Isle pattern from Chart C. Work even until Chart C is complete. Change to A. Work even until piece measures 1¾" (4.5 cm) from turning row, ending with a WS row. Break yarn; place sts on holder. Work second Leg. Do not break yarn.
Join Legs (RS): Work to last 2 sts of second leg, place marker (pm), CO 18 (22, 26) sts for crotch, work 2 sts from holder for first Leg, pm, work to end of first leg—92 (102, 112) sts. Work even for 1 row.

Shape Crotch (RS): Decrease 2 sts this row, then every other row 9 (10, 11) times, as follows: Work to first marker, slip marker (sm), ssk, work to 2 sts before next marker, k2tog, sm, work to end—72 (80, 88) sts remain. Work even, removing markers on first row, until piece measures 7 (8, 9)" [18 (20.5, 23) cm] from beginning of crotch, ending with a WS row, increase 2 sts evenly across last row—74 (82, 90) sts.
Shape Waistband (RS): Change to smaller needles and 2x2 Rib. Work even for 1¼" (3 cm), ending with a RS row. Knit 1 row (turning row). Work even in 2x2 Rib for 1¼" (3 cm), ending with a WS row. BO all sts in pattern.

BACK

Work as for Front until piece measures 6¾ (7¾, 8¾)" [17 (19.5, 22) cm] from beginning of crotch, ending with a WS row.
Shape Back
Note: Back is shaped using Short Rows (see Special Techniques, page 158). Work wraps together with wrapped sts as you come to them.
Row 1 (RS): Work 39 (43, 47) sts, wrp-t.
Row 2: Work 8 sts, wrp-t.
Row 3: Work to 6 (7, 8) sts past wrapped st of row before last row worked, wrp-t.
Repeat Row 3 seven times, work to end, working final wrap together with wrapped st. Work even for 1 row, increase 2 sts evenly across—74 (82, 90) sts. **(RS)** Shape waistband as for Front.

FINISHING

Block pieces to measurements. Fold Leg hem to WS at turning row and sew in place, being careful not to let sts show on RS. Sew side, crotch, and Leg seams. Measure elastic to fit snugly around baby's waist and add 1" (2.5 cm) for overlap. Using sewing needle and thread, sew ends of elastic together, overlapping 1" (2.5 cm). Fold waistband at turning row over elastic to WS, and sew in place, being careful not to let sts show on RS.

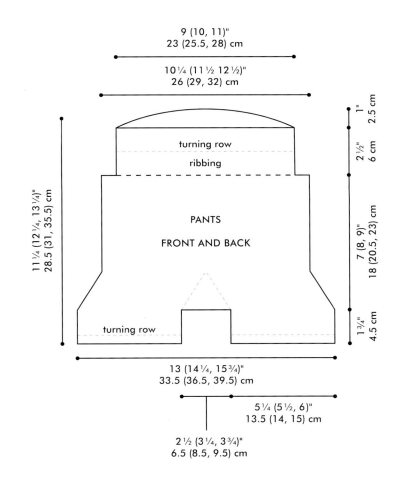

9 (10, 11)"
23 (25.5, 28) cm

10 ¼ (11 ½ 12 ½)"
26 (29, 32) cm

1"
2.5 cm

turning row

2 ½"
6 cm

ribbing

11 ¼ (12 ¼, 13 ¼)"
28.5 (31, 35.5) cm

PANTS

FRONT AND BACK

7 (8, 9)"
18 (20.5, 23) cm

1 ¾"
4.5 cm

turning row

13 (14 ¼, 15 ¾)"
33.5 (36.5, 39.5) cm

5 ¼ (5 ½, 6)"
13.5 (14, 15) cm

2 ½ (3 ¼, 3 ¾)"
6.5 (8.5, 9.5) cm

Maude Honeycomb Blanket

ALTHOUGH IT LOOKS COMPLICATED, THIS 1950S BLANKET IS DECEPTIVELY SIMPLE.
IT'S WORKED IN A SLIP STITCH PATTERN THAT REQUIRES THAT YOU HANDLE ONLY ONE COLOR AT A TIME.
I CHOSE A WONDERFULLY SOFT, LIGHT, AND SNUGGLY ORGANIC COTTON THAT'S DYED IN DELICATE COLORS
FOR THE BLANKET SHOWN HERE. FOR A COMPLETELY DIFFERENT EFFECT, YOU MIGHT TRY USING TWO
BRIGHT COLORS OR TWO DIFFERENT UNDYED COTTON SHADES.

FINISHED MEASUREMENTS
30" wide × 38" long (76 cm x 96.5 cm),
including Edging

YARN
Blue Sky Alpacas Dyed Cotton (100%
cotton; 150 yards [137 meters] / 100
grams): 5 hanks #606 Shell (MC), 4 hanks
#623 Toffee (A)

NEEDLES
One 24" (60 cm) long or longer circular
(circ) needle size US 9 (5.5 mm)
Change needle size if necessary
to obtain correct gauge.

GAUGE
18½ sts and 34½ rows = 4" (10 cm)
in Honeycomb Pattern

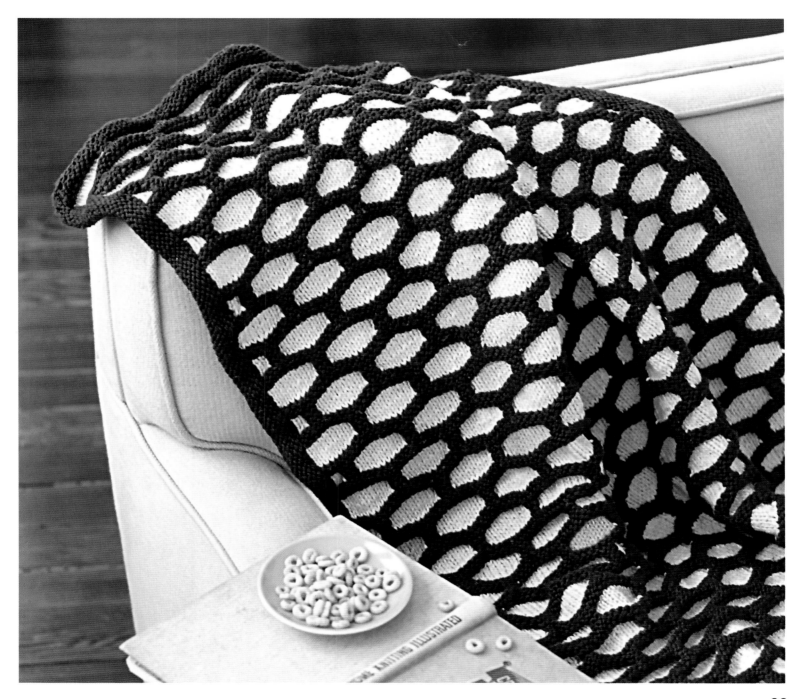

knitting in the 1940s

When Germany invaded Poland in 1939, Americans turned to charity knitting as they had during World War I. They knitted for soldiers as well as for injured civilians and refugees in Europe, including babies. Yarn companies lowered prices to help the relief effort, and even helped coordinate charity knitting with the Red Cross. They trained instructors and offered free knitting classes—not just a wise investment in the war effort but also a savvy way to create future knitters. This "relief knitting" led to a surge in baby knitting for charity. Bundles for Britain and Russian War Relief were just two of the efforts for which thousands of baby garments were knit.

Baby knitting was also on the rise for another reason: Wartime marriages and later postwar prosperity caused population growth in America to explode, doubling between 1946 and 1947 alone—and all those babies needed booties! National Baby Week in May 1943 prompted stores to release hundreds of new baby patterns. With the high birth rate, chilly fuel-rationed homes, and the shortage of rubber that was then used for diaper covers, wool garments for babies became even more popular, and in particular soakers became the must-have garment for any baby's layette. A frugal parent might make soakers from the recycled wool taken from an adult sweater. Even tiny scraps of wool were saved to make the Fair Isle garments that were popular at the time.

Wool shortages meant that wool was strictly rationed in America and Britain—but allowances were made for children's woolens, and in America, many women with wartime jobs had money and time to spend. Yarn manufacturers poured resources not only into war effort knitting, but into non-war knitting as well, using contests and other publicity stunts. Soon it became commonplace to see knitters everywhere.

KEY

- ☐ Knit on RS, purl on WS.
- ⊡ Purl on RS, knit on WS.
- ☑ Slip st purlwise wyib on RS and wyif on WS.
- ▨ MC
- ☐ A

HONEYCOMB PATTERN

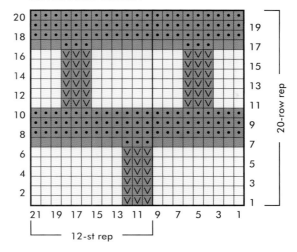

20-row rep

12-st rep

STITCH PATTERN

Honeycomb Pattern (multiple of 12 sts + 9; 20-row repeat) (see Chart)

Note: Slip all sts purlwise.

Row 1 (RS): Using MC, k9, *slip 3 wyib, k9; repeat from * to end.

Row 2: *P9, slip 3 wyif; repeat from * to last 9 sts, p9.

Rows 3-6: Repeat Rows 1 and 2.

Row 7: Change to A. K9, *p3, k9; repeat from * to end.

Rows 8-10: Work in Rev St st, beginning with a knit row.

Row 11: Change to MC. K3, slip 3 wyib, k3, *k6, slip 3 wyib, k3; repeat from * to end.

Row 12: *P3, slip 3 wyif, p6; repeat from * to last 9 sts, p3, slip 3 wyif, p3.

Rows 13-16: Repeat Rows 11 and 12.

Row 17: Change to A. K3, p3, k3, *k6, p3, k3; repeat from * to end.

Rows 18-20: Work in Rev St st, beginning with a knit row.

Repeat Rows 1-20 for Honeycomb Pattern.

BLANKET

Note: Slip all sts purlwise.

Work Bottom Edging: With A, CO 115 sts. Work in Rev St st (purl 1 row, knit 1 row) for 2 rows.

Increase Row (RS): P1, M1, purl to last st, M1, p1–117 sts. Work even for 3 rows. Repeat Increase Row once–119 sts. Work even for 1 row.

Set-Up Row (RS): Change to MC. K9, *slip 3 sts, k1, M1, k7; repeat from * to end–129 sts. Work Honeycomb Pattern: Work Rows 2-20 of Honeycomb Pattern once, Rows 1-20 fourteen times, then Rows 1-6 once (you may follow Chart or text for pattern).

Work Top Edging:

Set-Up Row (RS): Change to A. K9, *p3, k2tog, k7; repeat from * to end–119 sts remain. Work in Rev St st for 1 row.

Decrease Row (RS): P1, ssp, purl to last 3 sts, p2tog, p1–117 sts remain. Work even for 3 rows. Repeat Decrease Row once–115 sts remain. Work even for 2 rows. BO all sts.

FINISHING

Side Edging

With RS of Blanket facing, using A, beginning after Bottom Edging, and ending before Top Edging, pick up and knit approximately 1 st for every 2 rows along one side edge of Blanket. Work in Rev St st for 1 row.

Decrease Row (RS): P1, ssp, purl to last 3 sts, p2tog, p1–2 sts decreased. Work even for 3 rows. Repeat Decrease Row once–2 sts decreased. Work even for 2 rows. BO all sts. Repeat for opposite side edge.

Sew Edging together at corners, allowing edges to roll under. Block to measurements.

Daisy Soakers

WHO WOULDN'T WANT TO WEAR FANCY PANTS LIKE THESE? FROM A 1940S BRITISH PATTERN
LEAFLET CALLED *THE FRENCH BABY BOOK*, THESE SOAKERS CAN BE USED AS A CLOTH DIAPER COVER, OR JUST AS
CUTE SHORTS OVER A REGULAR DISPOSABLE DIAPER OR EVEN TRAINING PANTS. (IF YOU USE THEM AS A
CLOTH DIAPER COVER, BE SURE TO LANOLIZE THE SOAKERS FOLLOWING THE INSTRUCTIONS ON PAGE 29.) KEEP IN MIND
THAT CLOTH DIAPERS TEND TO BE BULKIER THAN DISPOSABLE DIAPERS, SO IF BABY IS WEARING DISPOSABLES YOU'LL
WANT TO MAKE THE PANTS A SIZE SMALLER. THE YARN IS A WONDERFUL ORGANIC TWO-PLY WOOL THAT
KNITS INTO A LIGHTWEIGHT BUT ABSORBENT FABRIC.

SIZES
6-12 months (12-18 months,
18-24 months)
Shown in size 18-24 months

FINISHED MEASUREMENTS
16½ (17½, 18½)" [42 (44, 47) cm] waist
19 (21½, 24½)" [48 (55, 62) cm] hips
8¾ (9, 9¼)" [22, 23, 23.5] cm long

YARN
Vermont Organic Fiber Company O-Wool
Classic 2-Ply (100% certified organic
Merino wool; 198 yards [181 meters] / 50
grams): 2 hanks #6510 Rose Gold

NEEDLES
One pair straight needles size
US 2 (2.75 mm)
One pair straight needles size
US 1 (2.25 mm)
Change needle size if necessary
to obtain correct gauge.

NOTIONS
1 yard (1 meter) 1" (2.5 cm) wide pajama
elastic; sewing needle and thread

GAUGE
26 sts and 34 rows = 4" (10 cm) in Stockinette stitch (St st), using larger needles
24 sts and 32 rows = 4" (10 cm) in
Chevron Pattern, using larger needles
32 sts and 36 rows = 4" (10 cm) in 2x2 Rib,
using smaller needles

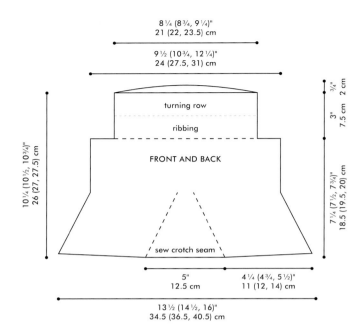

8 ¼ (8 ¾, 9 ¼)"
21 (22, 23.5) cm

9 ½ (10 ¾, 12 ¼)"
24 (27.5, 31) cm

¾"
2 cm

3"
7.5 cm

turning row

ribbing

FRONT AND BACK

10 ¼ (10 ½, 10 ¾)"
26 (27, 27.5) cm

7 ¼ (7 ½, 7 ¾)"
18.5 (19.5, 20) cm

sew crotch seam

5"
12.5 cm

4 ¼ (4 ¾, 5 ½)"
11 (12, 14) cm

13 ½ (14 ½, 16)"
34.5 (36.5, 40.5) cm

STITCH PATTERNS

Chevron Pattern (multiple of 8 sts + 1; 2-row repeat)

Row 1 (RS): *K1-f/b, k2, k3tog, k1, k1-f/b; repeat from * to last st, k1.

Row 2: Purl.

Repeat Rows 1 and 2 for Chevron Pattern.

2x2 Rib (multiple of 4 sts + 2; 1-row repeat)

Row 1 (RS): K2, *p2, k2; repeat from * to end.

Row 2: Knit the knit sts and purl the purl sts as they face you.

Repeat Row 2 for 2x2 Rib.

FRONT

Using larger needles, CO 32 sts. Begin St st. Work even for 2 rows.

(RS) Continuing in St st, using Cable CO (see Special Techniques, page 158), CO 25 (29, 33) sts at beginning of next 2 rows, working CO sts in St st—82 (90, 98) sts.

SIZES 6-12 MONTHS (18-24 MONTHS) ONLY

Establish Pattern (RS): Work in Chevron Pattern over next 25 (33) sts, place marker (pm) for crotch, work in St st over next 32 sts, pm, work in Chevron Pattern to end. Work even for 3 rows.

SIZE 12-18 MONTHS ONLY

Establish Pattern (RS): K2tog, k1, k1-f/b, work in Chevron Pattern over next 25 sts, pm for crotch, work in St st over next 32 sts, pm, work in Chevron Pattern over next 24 sts, k1-f/b, k1, k2tog, k1. Purl 1 row. Work even for 2 rows, working first 4 and last 5 sts of row as established.

ALL SIZES

Shape Crotch (RS): Decrease 1 st each side this row, then every other row 11 times, as follows: Work to first marker, slip marker (sm), ssk, work to 2 sts before second marker, sm, k2tog, work to end—58 (66, 74) sts remain. Work even for 1 row.

Next Row (RS): Work to first marker, remove marker, k3, k3tog, k1, k1-f/b, remove marker, work to end—57 (65, 73) sts remain. Work even, working Chevron Pattern across crotch sts, until piece measures 7¼ (7½, 7¾)" [18.5 (19.5, 20) cm] from the beginning, ending with a WS row.

Next Row (RS): Change to smaller needles and 2x2 Rib. Work even for 15 rows, increase 9 (5, 1) st(s) evenly spaced across first row—66 (70, 74) sts. Knit 1 WS row (turning row). Continuing in 2x2 Rib, work even for 14 rows. BO all sts in pattern.

BACK

Work as for Front to beginning of 2x2 Rib.

Next Row (RS): Change to smaller needles and 2x2 Rib. Work even for 2 rows, increase 9 (5, 1) st(s) evenly spaced across first row—66 (70, 74) sts.

Shape Back

Note: Back is shaped using Short Rows (see Special Techniques, page 158).

Row 1 (RS): Work to last 10 sts, wrp-t.

Row 2: Work 46 (50, 54) sts, wrp-t.

Row 3: Work 38 (42, 46) sts, wrp-t.

Row 4: Work 30 (34, 38) sts, wrp-t.

Row 5: Work 22 (26, 30) sts, wrp-t.

Row 6: Work 14 (18, 22) sts, wrp-t.

Work to end of row, working wraps together with wrapped sts as you come to them. Work 1 WS row, working remaining wrap.

Work even for 12 rows. Knit 1 WS row (turning row). Continuing in 2x2 Rib, work even for 14 rows. BO all sts in pattern.

FINISHING

Block pieces lightly to measurements. Sew side and crotch seams. Measure elastic to fit snugly around baby's waist and add 1" (2.5 cm) for overlap. Using sewing needle and thread, sew ends of elastic together, overlapping 1" (2.5 cm). Fold waistband at turning row over elastic to WS, and sew in place, being careful not to let sts show on RS.

Otto
Short-Sleeved
Pullover
&
Archie Vest

THE TRADITIONAL ART OF FAIR ISLE KNITTING, POPULARIZED IN BRITAIN BY THE PRINCE OF WALES IN 1927, EXPERIENCED A RESURGENCE IN THE 1940S. DURING THIS PERIOD OF WOOL SHORTAGES AND DEPRIVATION, STRANDED MULTICOLORED DESIGNS GAVE KNITTERS SOMETHING SPECIAL TO MAKE WITH WOOL LEFT OVER FROM OTHER PROJECTS OR YARN UNRAVELED FROM EXISTING GARMENTS. BOTH THE SHORT-SLEEVED PULLOVER AND THE VEST ARE WORKED FLAT, THEN STITCHES ARE PICKED UP AT THE NECK AFTER THE PIECE HAS BEEN SEWN TOGETHER. THESE 1947 PATTERNS ARE CHARTED HERE FOR EASE OF USE, ALTHOUGH CHARTS ARE RARE IN VINTAGE PATTERNS. INSTRUCTIONS WERE INSTEAD WRITTEN OUT LINE BY LINE, WITH LITTLE EXPLANATION OF TECHNIQUES. IF A KNITTER BECAME CONFUSED, HER BEST OPTION WAS TO ASK A FRIEND OR FAMILY MEMBER FOR HELP, OR HEAD TO THE LOCAL DEPARTMENT STORE OR YARN SHOP, WHERE YARN COMPANIES PAID EXPERT KNITTING INSTRUCTORS TO DOLE OUT ADVICE AT NO CHARGE.

Otto Short-Sleeved Pullover

SIZES
3-6 months (6-12 months)
Shown in size 6-12 months

FINISHED MEASUREMENTS
17 (20)" [43 (51) cm] chest

YARN
Hand Jive Nature's Palette Fingering Yarn
(100% Merino wool; 185 yards [169
meters] / 50 grams): 3 hanks Seafoam
(MC); 2 hanks Mallard (A)

NEEDLES
One pair straight needles
size US 1 (2.25 mm)
One pair straight needles
size US 2 (2.75 mm)
Change needle size if necessary
to obtain correct gauge.
One set of five double-pointed needles
(dpn) size US 2 (2.75 mm)

NOTIONS
Stitch marker

GAUGE
32 sts and 36 rows = 4" (10 cm)
in Fair Isle Pattern using larger needles

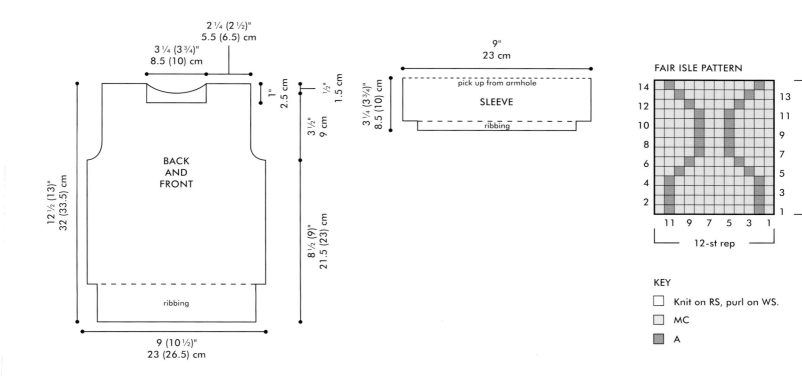

STITCH PATTERNS

2x2 Rib (multiple of 4 sts; 1-row/rnd repeat)
All Rows/Rnds: *K2, p2; repeat from * to end.

1x1 Rib (multiple of 2 sts; 1-row repeat)
All Rows: *K1, p1; repeat from * to end.

BACK

Using smaller needles and A, CO 72 (84) sts. Begin 2x2 Rib. Work even until piece measures 2" (5 cm) from the beginning.
Begin Fair Isle Pattern (RS): Change to larger needles and Fair Isle Pattern from Chart. Work even until piece measures 8½ (9)" [21.5 (23) cm] from the beginning, ending with a WS row.
Shape Armholes (RS): BO 3 (4) sts at beginning of next 2 rows, then decrease 1 st each side every other row 2 (3) times–62 (70) sts remain. Work

even until armhole measures 3½" (9 cm) from beginning of shaping, ending with a WS row.
Shape Neck and Shoulders (RS): Work 18 (20) sts, join a second ball of yarn, BO center 26 (30) sts, work to end. Working both sides at the same time, work even until armhole measures 4" (10 cm) from beginning of shaping, ending with a WS row. BO remaining sts.

FRONT

Work as for Back until armhole measures 3" (7.5 cm) from beginning of shaping, ending with a WS row. Shape neck and shoulders as for Back.

FINISHING

Block pieces to measurements. Sew shoulder seams.

Neckband: With RS facing, using dpn and A, pick up and knit 112 (120) sts around neck shaping. Join for working in the rnd; place marker for beginning of rnd. Begin 2x2 Rib. Work even for 9 rnds. BO all sts in pattern.

SLEEVES

With RS facing, using larger needles and MC, pick up and knit 72 sts around armhole edge. Begin Fair Isle Pattern from Chart, beginning with Row 2 of Chart. Work even until piece measures 2¾ (3¼)" [7 (8.5) cm] from the beginning, ending with a WS row. Change to smaller needles, A, and 1x1 Rib. Work even for 6 rows. BO all sts in pattern.

Sew side and Sleeve seams.

Archie Vest

SIZES
3-6 months (6-12 months,
12-18 months, 18-24 months)
Shown in size 3-6 months

FINISHED MEASUREMENTS
20 (21½, 23, 24½)" [51 (55, 58, 62) cm]

YARN
Hand Jive Nature's Palette Fingering Yarn
(100% Merino wool; 185 yards [169
meters] / 50 grams): 2 (2, 3, 3) hanks
Mallard (MC); 1 hank Seafoam (A)

NEEDLES
One pair straight needles
size US 1 (2.25 mm)
One pair straight needles
size US 2 (2.75 mm)
One set of five double-pointed needles
(dpn) size US 1 (2.25 mm)
Change needle size if necessary
to obtain correct gauge.

NOTIONS
Stitch marker

GAUGE
32 sts and 36 rows = 4" (10 cm)
in Fair Isle pattern using larger needles

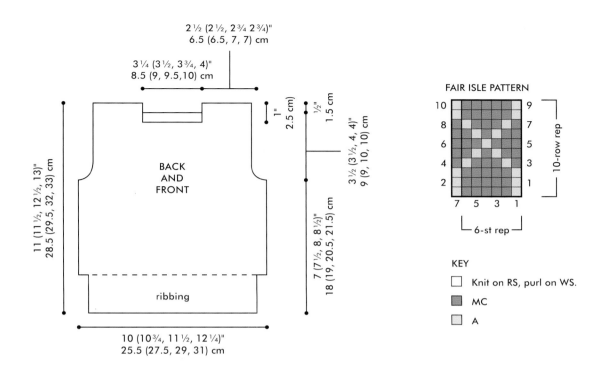

2 ½ (2 ½, 2 ¾ 2 ¾)"
6.5 (6.5, 7, 7) cm

3 ¼ (3 ½, 3 ¾, 4)"
8.5 (9, 9.5,10) cm

1"
2.5 cm

½"
1.5 cm

BACK
AND
FRONT

3 ½ (3 ½, 4, 4)"
9 (9, 10, 10) cm

11 (11 ½, 12 ½, 13)"
28.5 (29.5, 32, 33) cm

7 (7 ½, 8, 8 ½)"
18 (19, 20.5, 21.5) cm

ribbing

10 (10 ¾, 11 ½, 12 ¼)"
25.5 (27.5, 29, 31) cm

FAIR ISLE PATTERN

10-row rep

6-st rep

KEY

☐ Knit on RS, purl on WS.

▨ MC

☐ A

STITCH PATTERN

2x2 Rib (multiple of 4 sts + 2; 1-row repeat)

Row 1 (RS): K2, *p2, k2; repeat from * to end.

Row 2: Knit the knit sts and purl the purl sts as they face you.

Repeat Row 2 for 2x2 Rib.

BACK

Using smaller needles and MC, CO 78 (82, 90, 94) sts. Begin 2x2 Rib. Work even for 2" (5 cm), ending with a WS row, and increasing 1 (3, 1, 3) st(s) on last row–79 (85, 91, 97) sts.

Begin Fair Isle Pattern (RS): Change to larger needles. Begin Fair Isle pattern from Chart. Work even until piece measures 7 (7½, 8, 8½)" [18 (19, 20.5, 21.5) cm] from the beginning, ending with a WS row.

Shape Armholes (RS): BO 5 sts at beginning of next 2 rows, then decrease 1 st each side every other row 3 (4, 5, 6) times–63 (67, 71, 75) sts remain. Work even until armhole measures 3½ (3½, 4, 4)" [9 (9, 10, 10) cm] from beginning of shaping.

Shape Neck (RS): Work 19 (20, 21, 22) sts, join a second ball of yarn, BO 25 (27, 29, 31) sts, work to end. Working both sides at the same time, work even until armhole measures 4 (4, 4½, 4½)" [10.5 (10.5, 11.5, 11.5) cm] from beginning of shaping, ending with a WS row. BO all sts.

FRONT

Work as for Back until armhole measures 3 (3, 3½, 3½)" [7.5 (7.5, 9, 9) cm] from beginning of shaping, ending with a WS row.

Shape Neck (RS): Work 19 (20, 21, 22) sts, join a second ball of yarn, BO 25 (27, 29, 31) sts, work to end. Working both sides at the same time, work even until armhole measures same as for Back. BO all sts.

FINISHING

Block pieces to measurements. Sew right shoulder seam.

Neckband: With RS facing, using dpn and MC, pick up and knit 110 (118, 126, 130) sts along neck shaping. Join for working in the rnd; place marker for beginning of rnd. Begin 2x2 Rib. Work even for ¾" (2 cm). BO all sts in pattern.

Armhole Edging: With RS facing, using smaller needles and MC, pick up and knit 86 (86, 94, 94) sts along armhole edge. Begin 2x2 Rib. Work even for ¾" (2 cm). BO all sts in pattern. Sew side seams.

Hazel Cape

THROUGHOUT THE 1950S, A TIME OF RELATIVE PROSPERITY, CAPES, WHICH CALL FOR A
COMPARATIVELY LARGE AMOUNT OF YARN, COULD BE FOUND IN EVERY FASHIONABLE BABY'S WARDROBE.
FOR THIS VERSION, WHICH DATES BACK TO THE EARLY 1950S, I CHOSE A YARN WITH BEAUTIFUL
DRAPE AND STITCH DEFINITION MADE OUT OF MERINO WOOL AND SEACELL, A SEAWEED DERIVATIVE. AS WITH ALL
GARMENTS THAT TIE AT THE NECK, BE SURE TO USE ONLY WHEN BABY IS SUPERVISED, OR LEAVE THE TIES OUT.

SIZES
6-12 months
(12-18 months, 18-24 months)
Shown in size 6-12 months

FINISHED MEASUREMENTS
41¾ (45, 48¼)" [106 (114.5, 122.5) cm]
at bottom edge
27¾ (30¾, 33¾)" [70.5 (78, 85.5) cm]
at shoulders

YARN
Fleece Artist Sea Wool (70% Merino wool /
30% Seacell; 383 yards [350 meters] / 115
grams): 3 (4, 5) hanks Ruby Red

NEEDLES
One 32" (80 cm) circular (circ)
needle size US 3 (3.25 mm)
Change needle size if necessary
to obtain correct gauge.

NOTIONS
Stitch markers; 2 yards (2 meters) ⅝"
(1.5 cm) wide ribbon

GAUGE
24 sts and 50 rows = 4" (10 cm)
in Ridged Eyelet Pattern

STITCH PATTERN
**Ridged Eyelet Pattern (even number of sts;
14-row repeat)**
Row 1 (RS): Knit.
Row 2: Knit.
Row 3: *Yo, k2tog; repeat from * to end.
Rows 4, 5, 7, 9, 11, and 13: Knit.
Rows 6, 8, 10, 12, and 14: Purl.
Repeat Rows 1-14 for Ridged Eyelet Pattern.

BODY
CO 250 (270, 290) sts. Begin Garter st (knit
every row). Work even for 10 rows.
Set-Up Row (WS): K5, place marker (pm),
[p60 (65, 70), pm] 4 times, k5.
Begin Pattern (RS): K5 (edge sts, keep in Garter
st), work in Ridged Eyelet Pattern to last 5 sts, k5
(edge sts, keep in Garter st). Work even for 3 rows.

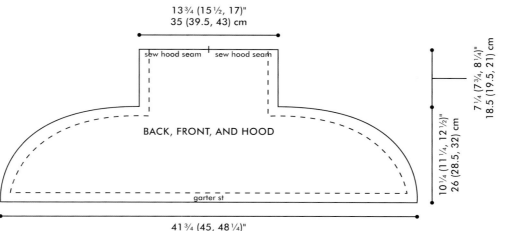

13¾ (15½, 17)"
35 (39.5, 43) cm

sew hood seam | sew hood seam

BACK, FRONT, AND HOOD

garter st

41¾ (45, 48¼)"
106 (114.5, 122.5) cm

7¼ (7¾, 8¼)"
18.5 (19.5, 21) cm

10¼ (11¼, 12½)"
26 (28.5, 32) cm

Shape Cape

Decrease Row 1 (RS): Continuing in pattern as established, knit to first marker, slip marker (sm), [knit to 2 sts before marker, k2tog, sm] 4 times, knit to end—246 (266, 286) sts remain. Work even for 1 row.

Decrease Row 2 (RS): Knit to first marker, sm, [k2tog, knit to marker, sm] 4 times, knit to end—242 (262, 282) sts remain. Work even for 1 row.

Repeat Decrease Row 1 once—238 (258, 278) sts remain. Work even for 1 row.

Repeat Decrease Row 2 once—234 (254, 274) sts remain. Work even for 1 row.

Repeat Decrease Row 1 once—230 (250, 270) sts remain. Work even for 1 row, removing markers.

Next Row (RS): Continuing in pattern as established, k7 (5, 6), pm, [k36 (40, 43), pm] 6 times, k7 (5, 6). Work even for 3 rows.

Decrease Row 3 (RS): Continuing in pattern as established, knit to first marker, sm, [k2tog, knit to marker, sm] 6 times, knit to end—224 (244, 264) sts remain. Work even for 1 row.

Decrease Row 4 (RS): Knit to first marker, sm, [knit to 2 sts before marker, k2tog, sm] 6 times, knit to end—218 (238, 258) sts remain. Work even for 1 row.

Repeat Decrease Row 3 once—212 (232, 252) sts remain. Work even for 1 row.

Repeat Decrease Row 4 once—206 (226, 246) sts remain. Work even for 1 row.

Repeat Decrease Row 3 once, removing markers as you come to them—200 (220, 240) sts remain. Work even until 5 (6, 7) vertical repeats of Ridged Eyelet Pattern have been completed. Repeat Rows 1-4 of Ridged Eyelet Pattern once.

Next Row (RS): Change to St st, keeping first and last 5 sts in Garter st as established. Work even for 7 rows.

Next Row (WS): K5, p1, pm, [p47 (52, 57), pm] 4 times, p1, k5.

Shape Shoulders

Next Row (RS): Continuing in St st, keeping first and last 5 sts in Garter st, decrease 4 sts this row, then every other row 4 times, as follows: Knit to first marker, sm, [k2tog, knit to marker, sm] 4

times, knit to end—180 (200, 220) sts remain. Work even for 3 rows, removing markers on first row.

Shape Neck

Decrease Row 1 (RS): K5, *k2tog; repeat from * to last 5 sts, k5—95 (105, 115) sts remain. Work even for 1 row.

Decrease Row 2 (RS): K5, [k15 (17, 19), k2tog] 5 times, k5—90 (100, 110) sts remain. Work even for 4 rows. Knit 1 row.

Eyelet Row (RS): K5, *yo, k2tog; repeat from * to last 5 sts, k5. Knit 1 row.

Hood

Row 1 (RS): Knit.

Row 2: K5, purl to last 5 sts, k5.

Row 3: K5, yo, k2tog, knit to last 7 sts, k2tog, yo, k5.

Row 4: Repeat Row 2.

Repeat Rows 1-4 fourteen (fifteen, sixteen) times. BO all sts.

FINISHING

Block piece to measurements. Sew seam at top of Hood. Thread ribbon through Eyelet Row at neck.

Bobby Kimono

KIMONO PATTERNS FOR BABY WERE VERY POPULAR WHEN THIS ONE
WAS ORIGINALLY PUBLISHED IN THE 1950S, IN KEEPING WITH THE GREAT INTEREST
IN ALL THINGS EASTERN AT THAT TIME. THE ORIGINAL WAS WORKED IN SEED
STITCH, BUT I CHOSE A DIMPLED SLIP STITCH INSTEAD TO MAKE A DENSER FABRIC.
THE PATTERN INCLUDES TWO VERSIONS—A LONG KIMONO (LIKE THE ONE
SHOWN HERE) THAT IS MEANT TO FIT VERY LOOSELY AND A SHORT ONE THAT FITS
MORE LIKE A STANDARD CARDIGAN. THE BODY OF THE GARMENT IS STILL COMPARATIVELY
WIDE, WHICH ALLOWS IT TO BE WORN FOR A LONG TIME, GRADUALLY
LOOKING SNUGGER AND SHORTER AS BABY GROWS.

SIZE
6-24 months

FINISHED MEASUREMENTS
22 ½" (57 cm) chest

YARN
Blue Sky Alpacas Hand Spun Organic Cotton (100% organic cotton; 132 yards [120 meters] / 68 grams): Long length 7 hanks; short length 5 hanks #60 Natural Cream

NEEDLES
One pair straight needles size US 3 (3.25 mm) Change needle size if necessary to obtain correct gauge.

NOTIONS
Crochet hook size US D-3 (3.25 mm); one 1" (25 mm) button

GAUGE
28 sts and 48 rows = 4" (10 cm) in Slip Stitch Pattern

NOTES
Kimono is worked in one piece from Back to Fronts. Two lengths are given; the long length is given first, with the short length following in parentheses. Where there is only one set of figures, it applies to both lengths.

STITCH PATTERN
Slip Stitch Pattern (multiple of 2 sts; 8-row repeat)
Row 1 (RS): *K1, slip 1 wyib; repeat from * to end [end k1 if an odd number of sts].
Row 2: Slip the slipped sts wyif and purl the purl sts.
Row 3: Knit.
Row 4: Purl.
Row 5: *Slip 1 wyib, k1; repeat from * to end [end k1 if an odd number of sts].
Row 6: Repeat Row 2.
Row 7: Knit.

Row 8: Purl.
Repeat Rows 1–8 for Slip Stitch Pattern.

KIMONO
Back
CO 112 (96) sts. Begin Garter st (knit every row). Work even for 10 rows. Change to Slip Stitch Pattern. Work even for 4 (6) rows.
LONG LENGTH ONLY
Shape Skirt (RS): Decrease 1 st each side this row, then every 12 rows 7 times–96 sts remain. Work even for 5 rows.
BOTH LENGTHS
Shape Waist (RS): Decrease 1 st each side this row, then every 6 rows 8 times–78 sts remain.

Work even until piece measures 15½ (8¼)" [39.5 (21) cm] from the beginning, ending with a WS row.

Sleeves
Next Row (RS): Using Cable CO (see Special Techniques, page 158), CO 19 sts at beginning of next two rows–116 sts. Working first and last 5 sts in Garter st and remaining sts in Slip Stitch Pattern, work even until piece measures 3¾" (9.5 cm) from Sleeve CO row, ending with a WS row.
Shape Back Neck (RS): Work 46 sts, join a second ball of yarn, BO center 24 sts for Back neck, work to end. Working both sides at the same time, work even for 1 row.

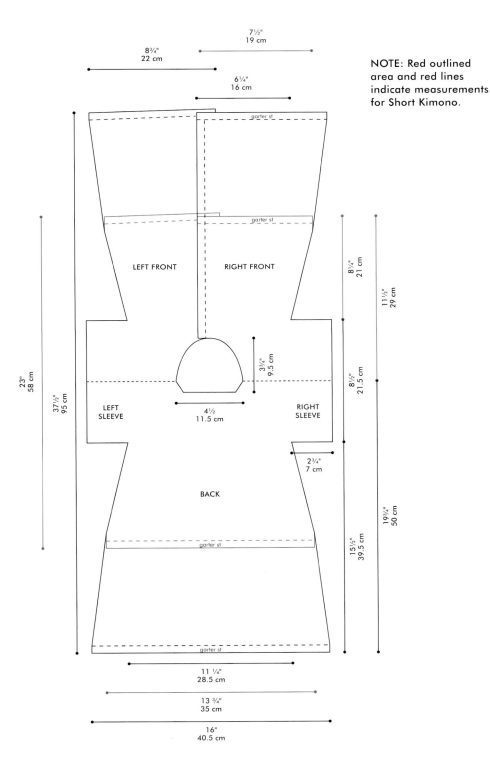

NOTE: Red outlined area and red lines indicate measurements for Short Kimono.

Next Row (RS): Decrease 1 st each neck edge this row, then every other row 3 times–42 sts remain each side. Work even until piece measures 2½" (6.5 cm) from beginning of Back neck shaping, ending with a WS row.

Shape Front Neck (RS): Using Cable CO, CO 2 sts at each neck edge 7 times, then 7 sts once–63 sts each side. Working 7 sts at each neck edge in Garter st, work even until piece measures 8½" (21.5 cm) from beginning of sleeve, ending with a WS row.

Fronts

Next Row (RS): BO 19 sts at beginning of next 2 rows–44 sts remain each side. Work even until piece measures 1½" (4 cm) from end of Sleeves, ending with a WS row.

Shape Waist (RS): Increase 1 st each side this row, then every 6 rows 8 times–53 sts each side. Work even for 11 (5) rows.

LONG LENGTH ONLY

Shape Skirt (RS): Increase 1 st each side this row, then every 12 rows 7 times–61 sts each side. Work even for 5 rows.

BOTH LENGTHS

Next Row (RS): Change to Garter st. Work even for 10 rows. BO all sts.

FINISHING

Block piece to measurements.

Collar: Beginning at right Front neck edge, pick up and knit 94 sts around neck shaping. Begin Garter st. Work even for 10 rows. BO all sts knitwise.

Sew side and Sleeve seams.

Button Closure: Using crochet hook, join yarn at base of Collar on Right Front. Work a crochet chain (see Special Techniques, page 158) long enough to fit around button snugly. Fasten off. Sew end of chain to right Front, in center of Collar to form a loop. Sew button to left Front, in center of Collar.

Harry Sailor Sweater

THIS SPORTY SAILOR-STYLE SWEATER DATES BACK TO 1946, WHEN THE MILITARY LOOK
FOR TOTS WAS VERY POPULAR. WORKED IN SOFT, LIGHTWEIGHT COTTON, IT IS PERFECT FOR SPRING AND SUMMER.
IT IS CONSTRUCTED IN FLAT PIECES, THEN AFTER THE PIECES ARE SEWN TOGETHER, SINGLE CROCHET IS
WORKED AROUND THE EDGES. I CHOSE TO ADD DECORATIVE STAR-SHAPED BAKELITE BUTTONS ON
THE POCKET AND COLLAR TO ACCENT THE PATRIOTIC THEME. IF YOU CHOOSE TO ADD BUTTONS AS WELL,
BE SURE TO SEW THEM ON SECURELY AND CHECK THEM REGULARLY TO MAKE SURE THEY
DO NOT LOOSEN AND BECOME A CHOKING HAZARD.

SIZES
6–12 months (12–18 months)
Shown in size 12-18 months

FINISHED MEASUREMENTS
20½ (22)" [52 (56) cm] chest

YARN
Rowan Yarns 4-Ply Cotton (100% cotton;
186 yards [170 meters] / 50 grams):
3 balls #150 Navy (MC); 1 ball #113
Bleached (A)

NEEDLES
One pair straight needles size US 2
(2.75 mm)
Change needle size if necessary
to obtain correct gauge.

NOTIONS
Crochet hook size US C-2 (2.75 mm); stitch
holders; three ½" (13 mm) buttons

GAUGE
32 sts and 48 rows = 4" (10 cm) in
Stockinette stitch (St st)

BACK
With MC, CO 82 (88) sts. Begin Garter st (knit every row). Work even for 8 rows.
Next Row (WS): K6 (edge sts, keep in Garter st), work in St st, beginning with a purl row, to last 6 sts, k6 (edge sts, keep in Garter st).
Work even until piece measures 2¾" (7 cm) from the beginning, ending with a WS row.
Next Row (RS): Change to St st across all sts. Work even until piece measures 7 (7½)" [18 (19) cm] from the beginning, ending with a WS row.

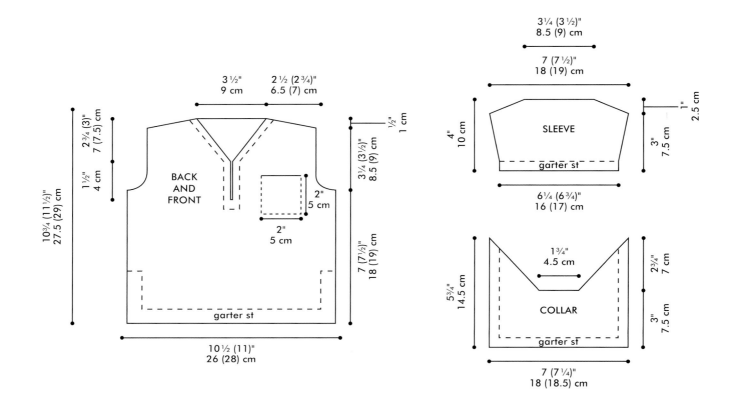

BACK AND FRONT

10¾ (11½)"
27.5 (29) cm

1½"
4 cm

2¾ (3)"
7 (7.5) cm

3½"
9 cm

2½ (2¾)"
6.5 (7) cm

½"
1 cm

3¼ (3½)"
8.5 (9) cm

7 (7½)"
18 (19) cm

2"
5 cm

2"
5 cm

garter st

10½ (11)"
26 (28) cm

SLEEVE

3¼ (3½)"
8.5 (9) cm

7 (7½)"
18 (19) cm

4"
10 cm

1"
2.5 cm

3"
7.5 cm

garter st

6¼ (6¾)"
16 (17) cm

COLLAR

5¾"
14.5 cm

1¾"
4.5 cm

2¾"
7 cm

3"
7.5 cm

garter st

7 (7¼)"
18 (18.5) cm

Shape Armholes (RS): BO 2 sts at beginning of next 2 rows, then decrease 1 st each side every other row 5 (6) times, as follows: K1, ssk, work to last 3 sts, k2tog, k1–68 (72) sts remain. Work even until armhole measures 3¼ (3½)" [8.5 (9) cm] from beginning of shaping, ending with a WS row.

Shape Shoulders (RS): BO 10 (11) sts at beginning of next 4 rows–28 sts remain. BO all sts.

POCKET LINING

With MC, CO 15 sts. Begin St st. Work even for 2" (5 cm), ending with a RS row. Place sts on holder.

FRONT

Work as for Back until piece measures 6 (6½)" [15 (16.5) cm] from the beginning, ending with a RS row.

Next Row (WS): Work 38 (41) sts, k6 (center panel, keep in Garter st), work to end of row. Work even for ½" (1.5 cm), working 6 center sts in Garter st, and ending with a WS row.

Shape Slit (RS): Work 41 (44) sts, join a second

ball of yarn, work to end. Working both sides at the same time, keeping 3 neck edge sts on each side in Garter st, and working armhole shaping as for Back when piece measures 7 (7½)" [18 (19) cm] from the beginning, work even until 37 (40) sts remain each side, ending with a WS row.

Shape Pocket Opening (RS): Continuing with armhole shaping, k1, ssk, k4, BO next 15 sts, work to end–21 (24) sts remain for left side; 36 (39) sts remain for right side.

Insert Pocket: Work to BO sts, with WS of Pocket Lining facing, work across Pocket Lining sts, work to end–36 (39) sts each side.

Next Row (RS): Continuing with armhole shaping, and keeping 3 neck sts on each side in Garter st, work even until armhole measures 1" (2.5 cm) from beginning of shaping, ending with a WS row.

Shape Neck (RS): Decrease 1 st at neck edge this row, then every other row 13 times, as follows: On left side, work to last 5 sts, k2tog, k3; on right side, k3, ssk, work to end—20 (22) sts remain each side for shoulders. Work even until armhole measures same as for Back to shoulder shaping, shape shoulders as for Back.

SLEEVES

With MC, CO 50 (54) sts. Begin Garter st. Work even for 5 rows.

Shape Sleeve (RS): Change to St st. Increase 1 st each side this row, then every 8 rows twice, as follows: K1, M1, work to last st, M1, k1—56 (60) sts. Work even until piece measures 3" (7.5 cm) from the beginning, ending with a WS row.

Shape Cap (RS): BO 3 sts at beginning of next 6 (8) rows, then 2 sts at beginning of next 6 (4) rows—26 (28) sts remain. BO all sts.

COLLAR

With MC, CO 56 (58) sts. Begin Garter st. Work even for 6 rows.

Next Row (WS): K6 (edge sts, keep in Garter st), work in St st, beginning with a purl row, to last 6 sts, k6 (edge sts, keep in Garter st). Work even until piece measures 3" (7.5 cm) from the beginning, ending with a WS row.

Shape Neck (RS): Work 21 (22) sts, join a second ball of yarn, BO center 14 sts, work to end—21 (22) sts remain each side. Working both sides at the same time, dec 1 st at each neck edge every row 8 times, then every other row 12 (13) times—1 st remains. Fasten off.

FINISHING

Block pieces to measurements. Sew Pocket Lining to WS of Front, being careful not to let

sts show on RS. Sew shoulder seams. Set in Sleeves. Sew side seams, beginning 2¾" (7 cm) above CO edge, leaving remaining side open. Sew Sleeve seams. With RS of Collar and Front facing, beginning at neck shaping on right neck edge, and beginning with fastened-off st on right side of Collar, sew Collar to neck shaping.

Body Edging: Using crochet hook and A, beginning at left side seam, work 1 rnd single crochet along entire bottom edge, including along both edges of side slits.

Sleeve Edging: Work as for Body Edging along each Sleeve cuff.

Pocket Edging: Work as for Body Edging across top of pocket opening.

Neck and Collar Edging: Work as for Body Edging around edges of neck slit and outside edges of Collar.

Sew one button to top center of pocket, and one to each back corner of Collar (see photos).

Monty Snowsuit with Cap & Mittens

THIS FOUR-PIECE SET DATES TO THE LATE 1950S. IT INCLUDES A CAP, MITTENS, PANTS, AND A JACKET, ALL WORKED IN WORSTED-WEIGHT YARN. THE RAGLAN SWEATER IS WORKED IN ONE PIECE ANDTHE PANTS ARE WORKED AS TWO TUBES IN THE ROUND. THE HAT AND MITTENS ARE WORKED IN THE ROUND AS WELL, ELIMINATING MOST OF THE SEAMING. UNLIKE TODAY, BEFORE THE 1960S, WORSTED-WEIGHT YARNS WERE RESERVED PRIMARILY FOR OUTDOOR GARMENTS. THE YARN I'VE USED HERE IS WASHABLE AND SOFT—PERFECT FOR LAYERING ON A CRISP WINTER DAY.

SIZES

SWEATER AND TROUSERS: 6-9 months (9-12 months, 12-18 months, 18-24 months)
CAP AND MITTENS: 6-9 months (9-12 months, 12-24 months)
Sweater and Trousers shown in size 18-24 months
Cap and Mittens shown in size 12-24 months

FINISHED MEASUREMENTS

SWEATER: 18 ½ (20 ¼, 22 ¼, 24)" [47 (51.5, 56.5, 61) cm] chest, buttoned
TROUSERS: 13 ½ (14 ½, 15 ½, 17 ½)" [34 (37, 39, 44) cm] waist, unstretched
CAP: 16 ¼ (17 ¼, 18 ¼)" [41.5 (44, 46.5) cm] circumference
MITTENS: 4 ¾ (5 ½, 6 ½)" [12 (14, 16.5) cm] palm circumference

YARN

Mission Falls 1824 Wool
(100% superwash Merino wool; 85 yards [78 meters] / 50 grams):
SWEATER: 5 (6, 7, 8) skeins;
TROUSERS: 4 (4, 5, 6) skeins;
CAP: 2 skeins;
MITTENS: 1 (1, 2) skeins #011 Poppy

NEEDLES

SWEATER: One 24" (60 cm) long circular (circ) needle size US 5 (3.75 mm)
One 24" (60 cm) long circular needle size US 3 (3.25 mm)
One set of five double-pointed needles (dpn) size US 5 (3.75 mm)
One set of five double-pointed needles size US 3 (3.25 mm)
TROUSERS: One pair straight needles size US 5 (3.75 mm)
One pair straight needles size US 3 (3.25 mm)
CAP: One set of five double-pointed needles size US 5 (3.75 mm)
MITTENS: One set of five double-pointed needles size US 5 (3.75 mm)
Change needle size if necessary to obtain correct gauge.

NOTIONS

SWEATER: Stitch markers; cable needle (cn); stitch holders; six ¾" (20 mm) buttons
TROUSERS: Cable needle (cn); 1 yard (1 meter) 1" (2.5 cm) wide elastic; sewing needle and thread

CAP: Stitch marker; pompom maker or 2 cardboard circles, each 2" (5 cm) diameter, for Pompom
MITTENS: Stitch marker; waste yarn

GAUGE
22 sts and 28 rows = 4" (10 cm) in Stockinette stitch (St st), using larger needles

NOTES
Sweater is worked from the top down. Trouser Legs are worked separately from cuff to waist with short-row shaping for the seat.

ABBREVIATION
C9: Slip next 3 sts to cn, hold to back, k3, hold cn to front, k3, k3 from cn.

STITCH PATTERNS
Cable Pattern (panel of 11 sts; 8-row repeat)
Rows 1, 3, and 5 (RS): P1, k9, p1.
Rows 2, 4, and 6: K1, p9, kl.
Row 7: P1, C9, p1.
Row 8: Repeat Row 2.
Repeat Rows 1-8 for Cable Pattern.

1x1 Rib (multiple of 2 sts; 1-row/rnd repeat)
Row/Rnd 1 (RS): *K1, p1; repeat from * to end [end k1 if an odd number of sts].
Row/Rnd 2: Knit the knit sts and purl the purl sts as they face you.
Repeat Row/Rnd 2 for 1x1 Rib.

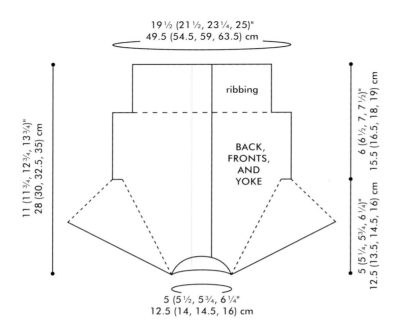

19 ½ (21 ½, 23 ¼, 25)"
49.5 (54.5, 59, 63.5) cm

ribbing

BACK,
FRONTS,
AND
YOKE

11 (11 ¾, 12 ¾, 13 ¾)"
28 (30, 32.5, 35) cm

6 (6 ½, 7, 7 ½)"
15.5 (16.5, 18, 19) cm

5 (5 ¼, 5 ¾, 6 ¼)"
12.5 (13.5, 14.5, 16) cm

5 (5 ½, 5 ¾, 6 ¼"
12.5 (14, 14.5, 16) cm

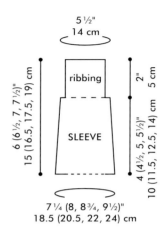

5 ½"
14 cm

ribbing

SLEEVE

6 (6 ½, 7, 7 ½)"
15 (16.5, 17.5, 19) cm

2"
5 cm

4 (4 ½, 5, 5 ½)"
10 (11.5, 12.5, 14) cm

7 ¼ (8, 8 ¾, 9 ½)"
18.5 (20.5, 22, 24) cm

NOTE: Pieces are worked from the top down.

SWEATER

Note: Piece is worked from the top down.

Yoke

With larger circ needle, CO 28 (30, 32, 34) sts.

Raglan Set-Up Row (RS): Begin St st, and place markers (pm) as follows: [k1, pm] twice, k4, pm, k1, pm, k14 (16, 18, 20), pm, k1, k4, [pm, k1] twice. *Note: The markers separate the Left Front, Left Sleeve, Back, Right Sleeve, and Right Front. The single sts between two markers are raglan "seam" stitches; these will later be counted as part of the Front or Back, when the Sleeves are separated from the Body.* Work even for 1 row.

Note: Raglan and neck shaping are worked at the same time. Cable pattern and buttonhole placement are begun after neck shaping is completed, but before raglan shaping is completed. Please read entire section through before beginning.

Shape Raglan (RS): Increase 8 sts this row, then every other row 15 (16, 18, 19) times, as follows: [Work to marker, M1, slip marker (sm), k1, sm, M1] 4 times, work to end–8 sts increased. AT THE SAME TIME, beginning on next RS row, **Shape Neck:** Continuing with raglan shaping, CO 3 sts at beginning of next 2 rows, 4 sts at beginning of next 2 rows, then 5 sts at beginning of next 2 rows.

Begin Cable Pattern (RS): Continuing with raglan shaping, k9, work Cable Pattern across next 11 sts, work to last 20 sts, work Cable Pattern across next 11 sts, k9.

Next Row (WS): K6 (edge sts, keep in Garter st [knit every row]), p3, work to last 9 sts, p3, k6 (edge sts, keep in Garter st).

Buttonhole Row (RS): Continuing with raglan shaping, k2, BO 2 sts, work to end.

Note: If working a girl's cardigan, work to last 4 sts, BO 2 sts, k2. Work even for 1 row, CO 2 sts over BO sts.

Work even until raglan shaping is complete, working additional buttonhole(s), every 1 ¾ (1 ⅞, 2, 2 ¼)" [4.5 (5, 5.5, 5.5) cm]–180 (190, 208, 218) sts [30 (31, 33, 34) sts each Front, 36 (38, 42, 44) sts each Sleeve, 48 (52, 58, 62) sts for Back]. Work even for 3 rows.

Next Row (RS): Work across 30 (31, 33, 34) sts and transfer to st holder for Left Front, work across next 36 (38, 42, 44) sts and transfer to st holder for Left Sleeve, work across next 48 (52, 58, 62) sts and transfer to st holder for Back, work to end of row. Transfer last 30 (31, 33, 34) sts to st holder for Right Front; do not break yarn–36 (38, 42, 44) sts remain for Right Sleeve.

Sleeves

With RS facing, using larger dpns, join separate ball of yarn at underarm, CO 2 (3, 3, 4) sts for underarm, pm for beginning of rnd, CO 2 (3, 3, 4) sts for underarm, work to end of rnd–40 (44, 48, 52) sts. Redistribute sts among 4 dpns [10 (11, 12, 13) sts each needle]. Begin St st (knit every rnd). Work even for 2 rnds.

Shape Sleeve

Decrease Rnd: Decrease 2 sts this rnd, then every 6 (4, 3, 3) rnds 3 (5, 7, 9) times, as follows: Work to 3 sts before marker, k2tog, k1, sm, k1, k2tog–32 sts remain. Work even until piece measures 4 (4½, 5, 5½)" [10 (11.5, 12.5, 14) cm] from underarm.

Repeat Decrease Rnd once–30 sts remain.

Next Rnd: Change to smaller dpns and 1x1 Rib. Work even for 2" (5 cm). BO all sts in pattern.

Body

Next Row (WS): With WS facing, transfer Right Front, Back, and Left Front sts to larger circ needle. Using yarn attached to Right Front, work across Right Front, pick up and purl 4 (6, 6, 8) sts from sts CO for right underarm, work across Back, pick up and purl 4 (6, 6, 8) sts from sts CO for left underarm, work to end–116 (126, 136, 146) sts. Work even until piece measures 3½ (4, 4½, 5)" [9 (10, 11.5, 12.5) cm] from underarm, working additional buttonholes as established, and ending with a WS row.

Decrease Row (RS): Work 25 (26, 23, 24) sts, *k2tog, k2; repeat from * to last 23 (24, 21, 22) sts, work to end–87 (95, 101, 109) sts remain.

Next Row (RS): Change to smaller circ needle. K6 (edge sts, keep in Garter st), work in 1x1 Rib to last 6 sts, k6 (edge sts, keep in Garter st). Work even for 2½" (6.5 cm), working 1 final buttonhole, and ending with a WS row. BO all sts in pattern.

Finishing

Collar: With WS facing, using larger circ needle, pick up and knit 16 (18, 20, 22) sts across sts CO for Back (including raglan "seam" sts). Begin St st, beginning with a knit row.

Shape Collar (WS): *Note: Collar will be folded over so that WS of collar faces RS of Cardigan.* Increase 6 sts at end of this row, then every row 5 times, as follows: Work to end of row, pick up and purl (on WS) or knit (on RS) 6 sts–52 (54, 56, 58) sts. *Note: The last st picked up on each side should be picked up from the center of the Front Garter st border.*

Next Row (RS): K3 (edge sts, keep in Garter st), work to last 3 sts, k3 (edge sts, keep in Garter st).

Increase Row (WS): Increase 5 sts evenly spaced across row–57 (59, 61, 63) sts. Work even until Collar measures 1½" (4 cm) from pick-up row, ending with a WS row.

Next Row (RS): Change to Garter st. Work even for 4 rows. BO all sts.

Block piece to measurements. Sew buttons opposite buttonholes.

TROUSERS

Left Leg

With smaller needles, CO 36, (40, 44, 50) sts. Begin 1x1 Rib. Work even for 2 (2½, 2½, 3)" [5 (6.5, 6.5, 7.5) cm], ending with a WS row.

Next Row (RS): Change to larger needles and St st, increase 15 sts evenly spaced across first row–51 (55, 59, 65) sts.

Begin Cable Pattern (WS): Work 20 (22, 24, 27) sts, work Cable Pattern across next 11 sts, beginning with Row 8 of Pattern, work to end. Work even until piece measures 9 (11, 12½, 13½)" [23 (28, 32, 34.5) cm] from the beginning, or to desired inseam length, ending with a WS row.

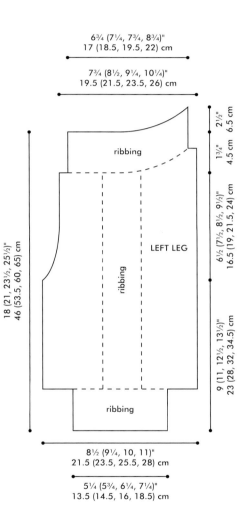

6¾ (7¼, 7¾, 8¾)"
17 (18.5, 19.5, 22) cm

7¾ (8½, 9¼, 10¼)"
19.5 (21.5, 23.5, 26) cm

2½"
6.5 cm

1¾"
4.5 cm

ribbing

6½ (7½, 8½, 9½)"
16.5 (19, 21.5, 24) cm

LEFT LEG

18 (21, 23½, 25½)"
46 (53.5, 60, 65) cm

ribbing

9 (11, 12½, 13½)"
23 (28, 32, 34.5) cm

ribbing

8½ (9¼, 10, 11)"
21.5 (23.5, 25.5, 28) cm

5¼ (5¾, 6¼, 7¼)"
13.5 (14.5, 16, 18.5) cm

Shape Crotch (RS): Decrease 1 st at end of this row, then every 8 rows 3 times, as follows: Work to last 3 sts, k2tog, k1–47 (51, 55, 61) sts remain. Work even until crotch measures 6½ (7½, 8½, 9½)" [16.5 (19, 21.5, 24) cm] from beginning of shaping, or to desired length to front waist, ending with a WS row.

Shape Seat

Note: Seat is shaped using Short Rows (see Special Techniques, page 158).

Row 1: K18 (20, 22, 23), wrp-t.
Row 2 and all WS Rows: Purl.
Row 3: K16 (18, 19, 20), wrp-t.
Row 5: K14 (15, 16, 17), wrp-t.
Row 7: K11 (12, 12, 13), wrp-t.
Row 9: K8 (8, 8, 9), wrp-t.
Row 11: K4, wrp-t.
Row 13: Work across all sts, working wraps together with wrapped sts as you come to them.
Shape Waistband (RS): Change to smaller needles and 1x1 Rib. Work even for 2½" (6.5 cm). BO all sts loosely in pattern.

Right Leg

Work as for Left Leg, reversing crotch shaping and working short-row seat shaping on WS rows instead of RS rows.

Finishing

Block pieces to measurements. Sew Legs together from back waistband, through crotch, to front waist band. Sew inseams. Measure elastic to fit snugly around baby's waist and add 1" (2.5 cm) for overlap. Using sewing needle and thread, sew ends of elastic together, overlapping 1" (2.5 cm). Fold waistband in half over elastic to WS, and sew in place, being careful not to let sts show on RS.

CAP

CO 90 (94, 100) sts. Join for working in the rnd, being careful not to twist sts; pm for beginning of rnd. Begin 1x1 Rib. Work even for 2½" (6.5 cm), increase 0 (1, 0) st(s) on last rnd–90 (95, 100) sts.
Decrease Rnd: *K3, k2tog; repeat from * to end–72 (76, 80) sts remain. Continuing in St st, work even until piece measures 6 (6½, 7)" [15 (16.5, 18) cm] from the beginning.
Shape Crown: *K2tog; repeat from * to end–36 (38, 40) sts remain.
Next Rnd: Change to 1x1 Rib. Work even for 12 rnds. Break yarn, leaving a long tail. Thread tail through remaining sts twice, pull tight and fasten off, with tail to WS.

Finishing

Block piece. Make one 2" (5 cm) Pompom (see Special Techniques, page 158). Attach to top of Cap.

MITTENS (both alike)

CO 24 (28, 32) sts. Join for working in the rnd, being careful not to twist sts; pm for beginning of rnd. Begin 1x1 Rib. Work even until piece measures 3 (3¼, 3½)" [7.5 (8.5, 9) cm] from the beginning, or to desired length to base of hand.
Next Rnd: Change to St st. Work even for 6 rnds.

SIZE 12-24 MONTHS ONLY

Thumb Opening

Next Rnd: Change to waste yarn. K6, slip these 6 sts back to left-hand needle, change to working yarn, knit these 6 sts again, work to end.

ALL SIZES

Work even until piece measures 4½ (4¾, 5)" [11.5 (12.5, 13) cm] from the beginning, or to 1¼" (3 cm) less than desired length.

Mitten Top

Rnd 1: *K4 (5, 6), k2tog; repeat from * to end–20 (24, 28) sts remain.
Rnd 2 and all Even-Numbered Rnds: Knit.
Rnd 3: *K3 (4, 5), k2tog; repeat from * to end–16 (20, 24) sts remain.
Rnd 5: *K2 (3, 4), k2tog; repeat from * to end–12 (16, 20) sts remain.
Rnd 7: *K1 (2, 3), k2tog; repeat from * to end–8 (12, 16) sts remain.
Rnd 9: *K2tog; repeat from * to end–4 (6, 8) sts remain.
Break yarn, leaving a long tail. Thread tail through remaining sts twice, pull tight and fasten off, with tail to WS.

SIZE 12-24 MONTHS ONLY

Thumb

Carefully remove waste yarn from Thumb sts and place bottom 6 sts and top 6 sts onto 3 dpns. Join yarn to bottom sts, pick up and knit 1 st in space between top and bottom sts, work across bottom sts, pick up and knit 1 st in space between bottom and top sts, work across top sts–14 sts. Join for working in the rnd; pm for beginning of rnd. Begin St st. Work even for 7 rnds.
Next Rnd: *K2tog; repeat from * to end–7 sts remain. Break yarn, leaving a long tail. Thread tail through remaining sts twice, pull tight and fasten off, with tail to WS.

Finishing

Block pieces to measurements.

Ducky Onesie

KNITTED ONESIES WERE CONSIDERED AN ESSENTIAL PART OF BABY'S WARDROBE
IN THE 1940S AND 1950S. THIS ONE-PIECE JUMPER WOULD HAVE BEEN WORKED IN SOFT BABY
WOOL WHEN IT WAS ORIGINALLY PUBLISHED IN THE LATE 1940S, BUT I'VE CHOSEN A
COOL COTTON PERFECT FOR SUMMER DAYS. I'VE ALSO ALTERED THIS PATTERN TO
INCLUDE EASY-ACCESS SNAPS ALONG THE BOTTOM.

SIZES
3-6 months (6-12 months)
Shown in size 6-12 months

FINISHED MEASUREMENTS
19½ (21)" [50 (53) cm] chest
20½ (22)" [52 (56) cm] hips

YARN
Dale of Norway Stork (100% cotton;
195 yards [178 meters] / 50 grams):
2 skeins #0003 Pastel Yellow (MC);
2 skeins #0002 Natural (A)

NEEDLES
One pair straight needles size US 1
(2.25 mm)
One pair straight needles size US 2
(2.75 mm)
Change needle size if necessary
to obtain correct gauge.

NOTIONS
Crochet hook size US B-1 (2.25 mm); stitch
holders; six ¼" (5 mm) buttons; 6" (15 cm)
snap tape, ⅜" (1 cm) wide; sewing needle
and thread; 3 colors of embroidery floss
for ducks; embroidery needle

GAUGE
32 sts and 44 rows = 4" (10 cm)
in Stockinette stitch (St st),
using larger needles

NOTE
When working stripes, do not break yarn
until stripes are complete; carry yarn not in
use up outside edge.

STITCH PATTERN

1x1 Rib (multiple of 2 sts; 1-row repeat)
Row 1 (RS): *K1, p1; repeat from * to end.
Row 2: Knit the knit sts and purl the purl sts as they face you.
Repeat Row 2 for 1x1 Rib.

BACK

Using larger needles and MC, CO 22 (24) sts. Begin Garter st (knit every row).
Shape Legs
Increase Row 1 (RS): Increase 1 st each side this row, then every row 17 (19) times, as follows: K1, M1, knit to last st, M1, k1–58 (64) sts.
Increase Row 2 (RS): Change to St st. Increase 2 sts each side this row, then every other row 5 times, as follows: [K1, M1] twice, knit to last 2 sts, [M1, k1] twice–82 (88) sts. Work even until piece measures 8¼ (8½)" [21 (21.5) cm] from the beginning, ending with a WS row.
Shape Waist (RS): Change to smaller needles, 1x1 Rib, and A, decrease 10 sts evenly spaced across row–72 (78) sts remain. Work even for 1 row. Continuing in 1x1 Rib, work 2 rows in MC, *2 rows in A, then 2 rows in MC. Repeat from * twice, increase 6 sts evenly across last row–78 (84) sts. Break MC.
Next Row (RS): Change to larger needles, St st, and A. Work even until piece measures 2¾ (3)" [7 (7.5) cm] from end of ribbing, ending with a WS row.
Shape Armholes (RS): BO 3 (4) sts at beginning of next 2 rows, then decrease 1 st each side every other row 4 times–64 (68) sts remain. Work even until armhole measures 3¼ (3½)" [8.5 (9) cm] from beginning of shaping, ending with a WS row.

Shape Shoulders and Neck (RS): BO 6 (7) sts at beginning of next 4 rows, then 7 sts at beginning of next 2 rows–26 sts remain. Place sts on holder for Neckband.

FRONT

Work as for Back until armhole measures 2¼ (2½)" [5.5 (6.5) cm] from beginning of shaping, ending with a WS row.
Shape Neck (RS): Work 22 (24) sts, join a second ball of yarn, BO center 20 sts, work to end. Working both sides at the same time, work even for 1 row. Decrease 1 st at each neck edge every other row 3 times–19 (21) sts remain each side for shoulders. Work even until armhole measures same as for Back to shoulder shaping, shape shoulders as for Back.

SLEEVES

Using smaller needles and MC, CO 52 (56) sts. Begin 1x1 Rib. Work even for 2 rows. Continuing in 1x1 Rib, work 2 rows in A, then 2 rows in MC, increase 6 sts evenly on last row–58 (62) sts. Break MC.
Next Row (RS): Change to larger needles, St st, and A. Work even until piece measures 2½" (6.5 cm) from the beginning, ending with a WS row.
Shape Cap (RS): BO 3 sts at beginning of next 4 rows, then 2 sts at beginning of next 14 rows–18 (22) sts remain. BO all sts.

FINISHING

Block pieces to measurements.
Crochet Front Shoulder Edging:
Row 1: With RS facing, using crochet hook and A, work 17 (19) singele crochet (sc) across BO shoulder edge.
Row 2: Ch 1, turn, sc in next 3 (4) sts, *ch 1, skip 1 sc for buttonhole, sc in next 4 sts; repeat from * once, ch 1, skip 1 sc for buttonhole, sc in next 3 (4) sts.

Row 3: Ch 1, turn, sc to end. Fasten off. Repeat for opposite shoulder.
Crochet Back Shoulder Edging: With RS facing, using crochet hook and A, work 17 (19) sc across BO shoulder edge. Work 2 rows sc. Fasten off. Repeat for opposite shoulder
Front Neckband: With RS facing, using smaller needles and MC, pick up and knit 4 sts along left edge of Left Shoulder Edging, 48 sts along Front neck shaping, and 4 sts along right edge of Right Shoulder Edging–56 sts. Begin 1x1 Rib. Work even for 1 row.
Buttonhole Row (RS): Change to A. K1, p1, yo, p2tog, work to last 3 sts, yo, k2tog, p1. Work even for 1 row. Change to MC. Work even for 1 row. BO all sts in pattern.
Back Neckband: With RS facing, using smaller needles and MC, pick up and knit 4 sts along left edge of Right Shoulder Edging, 26 sts across Back neck, and 4 sts along right edge of Left Shoulder Edging–34 sts. Work as for Front Neckband, omitting buttonholes.
Crochet Crotch Edging: With RS facing, using crochet hook and MC, work 20 (22) sc across CO edge of crotch. Work 2 rows sc. Fasten off. Sew side seams.
Leg Edging: With RS facing, using larger needles and MC, pick up and knit 4 sts along edge of Crochet Crotch Edging, 64 (68) sts around leg opening, then 4 sts along edge of Crochet Crotch Edging–72 (76) sts. Begin 1x1 Rib. Work even for ¾" (2 cm). BO all sts in pattern. Repeat for opposite leg.
Set in Sleeves. Sew Sleeve seams. Using sewing needle and thread, sew one half of snap tape to RS of Back crotch; sew other half of snap tape to WS of Front crotch.

Using embroidery needle and floss, embroider 5 ducks across Front chest (see photo and illustration).

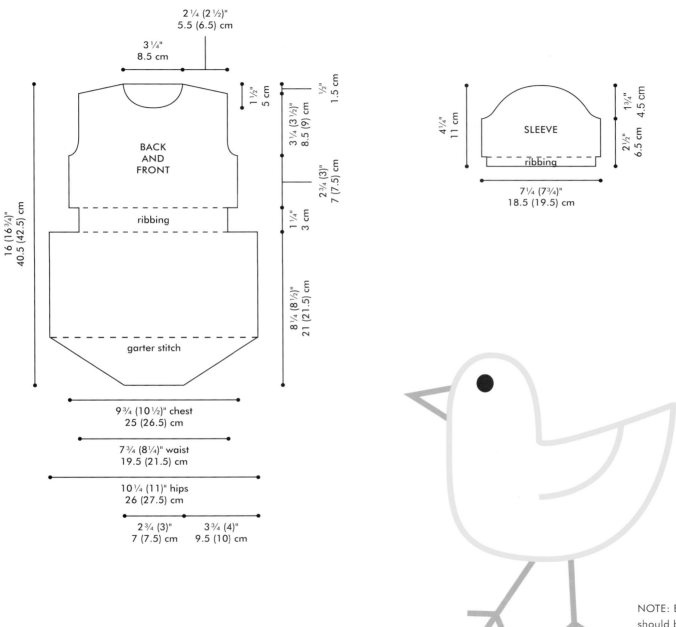

2 ¼ (2 ½)"
5.5 (6.5) cm

3 ¼"
8.5 cm

1 ½"
5 cm

½"
1.5 cm

3 ¼ (3 ½)"
8.5 (9) cm

BACK
AND
FRONT

2 ¾ (3)"
7 (7.5) cm

1 ¼"
3 cm

ribbing

16 (16 ¾)"
40.5 (42.5) cm

8 ¼ (8 ½)"
21 (21.5) cm

garter stitch

9 ¾ (10 ½)" chest
25 (26.5) cm

7 ¾ (8 ¼)" waist
19.5 (21.5) cm

10 ¼ (11)" hips
26 (27.5) cm

2 ¾ (3)"
7 (7.5) cm

3 ¾ (4)"
9.5 (10) cm

SLEEVE

4 ¼"
11 cm

1 ¾" 4.5 cm

2 ½"
6.5 cm

ribbing

7 ¼ (7 ¾)"
18.5 (19.5) cm

NOTE: Embroidered ducks
should be approximately
1 ¼" (3 cm) square.

Frankie Striped Socks

ALTHOUGH THIS POSTWAR PATTERN FEATURED SOLID-COLORED SOCKS, I DECIDED TO ADD STRIPES, WHICH WERE ACTUALLY MORE TYPICAL OF FRUGAL KNITTING IN THE 1940S. BACK THEN, BABY SOCKS WOULD HAVE BEEN MADE FROM SCRAPS FROM OTHER PROJECTS, OR EVEN FROM RECYCLED WOOL UNPICKED FROM AN OLD ADULT SWEATER. UNUSUAL COLOR COMBINATIONS BECAME COMMONPLACE AS KNITTERS MADE FRUGALITY A FASHION STATEMENT. BITS OF MORE COLORFUL YARNS LEFT OVER FROM BEFORE THE WAR EFFORT BRIGHTENED UP THE DULL MILITARY COLORS OF YARN SO PREVALENT IN EVERY SHOP DURING THE WAR.

SIZES
6-12 months (12-18 months)
Shown in size 6-12 months

FINISHED MEASUREMENTS
Foot circumference: 5½ (6)" [14 (15) cm]
Foot length: 4½ (5)" [11.5 (12.5) cm]

YARN
Hand Jive Nature's Palette Fingering Yarn (100% Merino wool; 185 yards [169 meters] / 50 grams): 1 hank each MC and A, in the following colorways: (clockwise, beginning at top) Chocolate (MC) and Coral (CC); Indian Paintbrush (MC) and Autumn Leaf (A); Lupine (MC) and Spring Grass (A); Zinfandel (MC) and Hydrangea (A); Coral Bells (MC) and Spring Grass (A)

NEEDLES
One set of four double-pointed needles (dpn) size US 1 (2.25 cm) Change needle size if necessary to obtain correct gauge.

NOTIONS
Stitch marker; stitch holder

GAUGE
32 sts and 40 rnds = 4" (10 cm) in Stripe Pattern

NOTE
When working Stripe Pattern, do not break yarn; carry unused color loosely up inside of Sock.

knitting in the 1950s

In the years following World War II, knitting was more popular than ever. The economy was booming, and millions of wartime charity knitters again turned to projects for themselves—and for their new babies, who were arriving in record-breaking numbers. Postwar and 1950s women married younger, worked less, enjoyed more prosperity, and had almost twice as many children as the previous generation had twenty years before. The media made an icon of the stay-at-home mother. Yarn companies aggressively strove to cater to the "modern woman," whose relative wealth gave her plenty of free time and disposable income to spend on yarn and knitting accoutrements.

The enthusiasm for knitting that had started twenty years before continued unabated into the 1950s. Pattern booklets proliferated. There was a staggering increase in the publication of patterns "for the whole family."

Yarn companies featured a bewildering variety of choices for the well-dressed baby's layette: crisp argyles, lively striped sets, and fancy Norwegian-style pullovers; frilly cardigans called "sacques"; tiny cabled or lace-stitch booties; hats in every imaginable color, material, and shape; and countless variations on the ever-present layette set. While many mothers opted for the newly available disposable diaper, wool soakers continued to be a staple in baby's wardrobe.

The department store knitting section and the yarn shop remained a friendly place for the knitter throughout the 1950s. Knitting instructors continued to provide the same advice and camaraderie that they had during the war years. For the first time, some shops turned to a novel self-serve model, which allowed knitters to touch the yarn and make their selections themselves. The selection of

yarn exploded in the 1950s, in part because of the proliferation of newly available nylon and acrylic fibers. But virgin wool remained the most popular yarn, and soft cottons made a comeback as favored yarns for baby wear. In both nylon and acrylics, new synthetic dyes presented a dazzling array of colors.

Yet despite these advances, as the 1950s came to a close and as modern convenience became the hallmark of the era, interest in knitting began to wane. Yarn companies shifted their focus to simpler beginner patterns and thicker, quick-to-knit yarns. While patterns for babies continued to be published, they lacked the extraordinary selection that knitters had enjoyed a few years earlier. Just as the world was poised for a change in 1959, so was the knitting industry. What may have been the golden age of vintage baby knits was ending.

STITCH PATTERNS

1x1 Rib (multiple of 2 sts; 1-rnd repeat)
All Rnds: *K1, p1; repeat from * to end.
Stripe pattern (any number of sts; 8-rnd repeat)
Rnd 1: With A, knit.
Rnd 2: Slip 1, knit to end.
Rnds 3 and 4: Knit.
Rnd 5: Change to MC. Knit.
Rnds 6-8: Repeat Rnds 2-4.
Repeat Rnds 1–8 for Stripe Pattern.

SOCK

Cuff

With MC, CO 48 (52) sts; divide evenly among 3 dpns. Join for working in the rnd, being careful not to twist sts; place marker (pm) for beginning of rnd. Begin 1x1 Rib. Work even for 1¼ (1½)" [3 (4) cm], decreasing 4 sts evenly spaced on last rnd–44 (48) sts remain.
Next Rnd: Change to Stripe Pattern. Work even for 12 rows. Break A.

Heel

Continuing with MC, k22 (24) sts onto 1 needle for instep to be worked later– 22 (24) sts remain. Change to working back and forth in rows.
Row 1 (RS): Slip 1, knit to end.
Row 2: Slip 1, purl to end.
Work even until Heel measures 1¼ (1½)" [3 (4) cm], ending with a WS row.

Turn Heel

Set-Up Row 1: K12 (13), ssk, k1, turn.
Set-Up Row 2: Slip 1, p3, p2tog, p1, turn.
Row 1: Slip 1, knit to 1 st before gap, ssk (the 2 sts on either side of gap), k1, turn.
Row 2: Slip 1, purl to 1 st before gap, p2tog (the 2 sts on either side of gap), p1, turn.
Repeat Rows 1 and 2 three times, omitting the final k1 and p1 sts in the last repeat for size 6-12 months–12 (14) sts remain.

Gusset and Foot

Using first needle, work across Heel sts, then with same needle, pick up and knit 9 (11) sts along left side of Heel flap; using second needle, work across 22 (24) sts of instep; using third needle, pick up and knit 9 (11) sts along right side of Heel flap, then with same needle, k6 (7) from first needle; pm for new beginning of rnd–52 (60) sts. Knit 1 rnd.

Decrease Rnd: On first needle, work across to last 3 sts, k2tog, k1; work across second needle; on third needle, k1, ssk, work to end–50 (58) sts. Knit 1 rnd.
Next Rnd: Change to Stripe Pattern. Work Decrease Rnd every other rnd 3 (5) times–44 (48) sts remain.
Work even until foot measures 3 (3½)" [7.5 (9) cm] from back of Heel. Break A.

Toe

Decrease Rnd: On first needle, work across to last 3 sts, k2tog, k1; on second needle, k1, ssk, work to last 3 sts, k2tog, k1; on third needle, k1, ssk, work to end–40 (44) sts remain. Knit 1 rnd. Work Decrease Rnd every other rnd 6 (7) times–16 sts remain. With third needle, knit across sts on first needle.

Break yarn, leaving a 10" (25.5 cm) tail. Graft sts together using Kitchener st (see Special Techniques, page 158).

Jackie Cabled Set

THE POPULARITY OF THE LAYETTE SET AS A BABY GIFT DATES BACK TO TIMES WHEN CHILLY HOMES MEANT BABIES TRULY NEEDED KNITS TO KEEP WARM. THIS SET INCLUDES A CARDIGAN AND BOOTIES MADE FROM A FINGERING-WEIGHT MERINO YARN, AS WELL AS A MATCHING BLANKET WORKED IN A LIGHT WORSTED-WEIGHT MERINO YARN. THE SIMPLE CABLES FEATURED ON THIS SET ARE SET AGAINST A GARTER-STITCH BACKGROUND RATHER THAN THE MORE COMMON REVERSE STOCKINETTE STITCH.

Jackie Cabled Blanket

FINISHED MEASUREMENTS
28" wide x 37½" long (71 x 95 cm)

YARN
Pear Tree 8-Ply Merino (100% Australian Merino wool; 215 yards [196 meters] / 100 grams): 6 hanks Robin's Egg

NEEDLES
One 32" (80 cm) long circular (circ) needle size US 7 (4.5 mm)
Change needle size if necessary to obtain correct gauge.

NOTIONS
Cable needle (cn); stitch markers

GAUGE
26 sts and 28 rows = 4" (10 cm) in Cable Pattern B

BLANKET
CO 146 sts. Begin Garter st (knit every row). Work even for 2" (5 cm), increase 30 sts evenly across last row—176 sts.
Begin Cable Pattern (WS): Work 10 sts in Garter St, place marker (pm), work Cable Pattern B from Chart to last 10 sts, pm, work in Garter st to end. Work even until piece measures approximately 35½" (90 cm) from the beginning, ending with Row 11 of Chart.
(RS) Change to Garter st. Work even for 2" (5 cm), decrease 30 sts evenly across first row—146 sts remain. BO all sts.

FINISHING
Block lightly.

Jackie Cabled Booties

SIZES
3-6 months (6-9 months, 9-18 months, 18-24 months, 2-3 years)
Shown in size 9-18 months

FINISHED MEASUREMENTS
3¾ (4¼, 4¾, 5¼, 5¾)" [9.5 (11, 12, 13.5, 14.5) cm] foot length
Note: Length is with Bootie folded flat. When worn, some of the length will be taken up by the width of the toes and ankle. Work a size that is slightly smaller than the actual foot length.

YARN
Pear Tree 4-Ply Wool (100% Australian Merino wool; 350 yards [320 meters] / 100 grams): 1 hank Robin's Egg
Note: Booties use approximately 135 (175, 200, 245, 295) yards [124 (158, 183, 223, 226) meters] per pair.

NEEDLES
One pair straight needles size US 3 (3.25 mm)
One pair straight needles size US 4 (3.5 mm)
Change needle size if necessary to obtain correct gauge.

NOTIONS
Cable needle (cn); stitch holders

GAUGE
32 sts and 35 rows = 5" (12.5 cm) in Cable Pattern A

NOTES
Booties are worked from the cuff down to the ankle. The leg sts are then placed on holders and the instep is worked to the toe. Stitches are then picked up along the sides of the instep and base of the leg, and worked for the sole. The Bootie is sewn together at the back of the leg and center of the sole.

BOOTIE
Leg
Using small needles, CO 44 (48, 52, 56, 60) sts. Begin Garter st (knit every row). Work even for 10 rows.
Begin Cable Pattern (WS): Change to larger needles. Work 2 (4, 6, 8, 10) sts in Garter st, work Cable Pattern A from Chart over 40 sts, work in Garter st to end. Work even until piece measures 3 (3¼, 3½, 3¾, 4)" [7.5 (8.5, 9, 9.5, 10) cm] from the beginning, ending with a WS row.

Instep
Next Row (RS): Work 16 (17, 18, 19, 20) sts and place on holder for right side of Leg, work 12 (14, 16, 18, 20) sts for Instep; place remaining 16 (17, 18, 19, 20) on holder for left side of Leg. Working only on Instep sts, continuing in pattern as established work even for 1½ (1¾, 2, 2¼, 2½)" [4 (4.5, 5, 5.5, 6.5) cm], ending with a WS row. Break yarn.

Sole
Next Row (RS): With RS facing, work across sts on holder for right side of Leg, pick up and knit 7 (8, 10, 12, 14) sts along right side edge of Instep sts, work across Instep sts, pick up and knit 7 (8, 10, 12, 14) sts along left side edge of Instep sts, work across sts on holder for left side of Leg—58 (64, 72, 80, 88) sts. Begin Garter st. Work even for 14 (16, 18, 20, 22) rows. BO all sts.

FINISHING
Sew back of leg and sole seams.

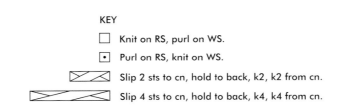

□ Knit on RS, purl on WS.

· Purl on RS, knit on WS.

Slip 2 sts to cn, hold to back, k2, k2 from cn.

Slip 4 sts to cn, hold to back, k4, k4 from cn.

CABLE PATTERN A

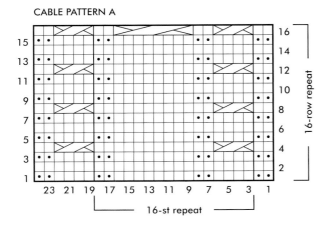

CABLE PATTERN B

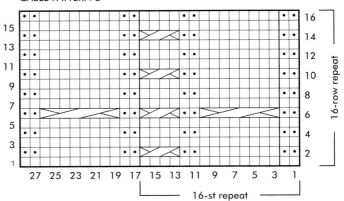

Jackie Cabled Cardigan

SIZES

6-12 months (12-18 months, 18-24 months)
Shown in size 6-12 months

FINISHED MEASUREMENTS

21 ½ (22 ½, 24)" [55 (57, 61) cm] chest, buttoned

YARN

Pear Tree 4-Ply Wool (100% Australian Merino wool; 350 yards [320 meters] / 100 grams): 2 (3, 3) hanks Robin's Egg

NEEDLES

One pair straight needles size US 4 (3.5 mm)
Change needle size if necessary to obtain correct gauge.

NOTIONS

Cable needle (cn); five (six, six) ¾" (20 mm) buttons

GAUGE

32 sts and 35 rows = 5" (12.5 cm) in Cable Pattern A

NOTE

Cardigan is worked in one piece from Back to Fronts.

STITCH PATTERN

1x1 Rib (multiple of 2 sts; 1-row repeat)
Row 1 (RS): *K1, p1; repeat from * to end [end k1 if an odd number of sts].
Row 2: Knit the knit sts and purl the purl sts as they face you.
Repeat Row 2 for 1x1 Rib.

BACK

CO 68 (72, 76) sts. Begin Garter st (knit every row). Work even for 10 rows.
Begin Cable Pattern (WS): Work 4 (0, 2) sts in St st, work Cable Pattern A from Chart over 60 (72, 72) sts, beginning with st# 18 (24, 24) of Chart, working from left to right and ending with st# 7 (1, 1), work 4 (0, 2) sts in St st. Work even until piece measures 8¼ (8¾, 9¼)" [21 (22, 23.5) cm] from the beginning, ending with a WS row.

SLEEVES

Next Row (RS): Using Cable CO (see Special Techniques, page 158), CO 34 (36, 40) sts at beginning of next 2 rows–136 (144, 156) sts. Working first and last 0 (4, 0) sts in St st, and remaining 34 (32, 40) CO sts in Cable Pattern as established, work even until Sleeves measure 3½ (4, 4½)" [9 (10, 11.5) cm] from Sleeve CO edge, ending with a WS row.
Shape Back Neck (RS): Work 54 (58, 64) sts, join a second ball of yarn, BO 28 sts for Back neck, work to end. Working both sides at the same time, work even for 1 (1¼, 1½)" [2.5 (3, 4) cm], ending with a WS row.
Shape Front Neck (RS): Using Cable CO, CO 18 sts at each neck edge–72 (76, 82) sts each side. Working first 6 CO sts at each neck edge in Garter st, and remaining 12 CO sts in Cable Pattern as established, work even for 4 rows.

Buttonhole Row (RS): Work to last 4 sts on Right Front, BO 2 sts, work to end of Left Front.
Next Row (WS): Work to BO sts, CO 2 sts over BO sts. Work 4 (5, 5) additional buttonholes, working 1 every 2¼" [5.5 cm], and working last buttonhole before working final Garter st edging. Work even until piece measures 3 (3½, 3¾)" [7.5 (9, 9.5) cm] from Front neck CO edge, ending with a WS row.

FRONTS

Next Row (RS): BO 34 (36, 40) sts at beginning of next 2 rows–38 (40, 42) sts remain each side.
Next Row (WS): Working first 4 (0, 2) sts of Right Front and last 4 (0, 2) sts of Left Front in St st, work even until piece measures 7 (7½, 8)" [18 (19, 20.5) cm] from BO edge of Sleeve, ending with a WS row.
Next Row (RS): Change to Garter st. Work even for 10 rows. BO all sts.

CUFFS

With RS facing, pick up and knit 3 sts for every 4 rows along cuff edge of Sleeve. Begin Garter st. Work even for 10 rows. BO all sts.

COLLAR

With RS facing, pick up and knit 76 sts along neck edge. Begin Garter st. Work even for 1 row.
Shape Collar (RS): Increase 1 st each side this row, then every other row 14 times, as follows: K1, M1, work to last stitch, M1, k1–106 sts. BO all sts.

FINISHING

Block piece to measurements. Sew side and Sleeve seams. Sew buttons opposite buttonholes.

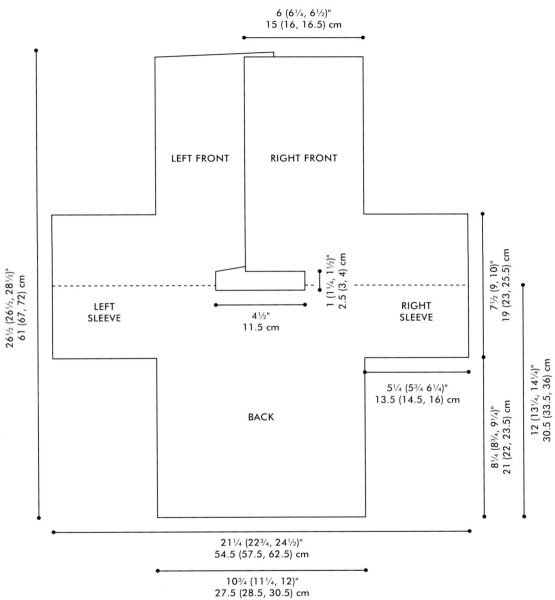

6 (6¼, 6½)"
15 (16, 16.5) cm

LEFT FRONT

RIGHT FRONT

26½ (26½, 28½)"
61 (67, 72) cm

LEFT
SLEEVE

RIGHT
SLEEVE

7½ (9, 10)"
19 (23, 25.5) cm

1 (1¼, 1½)"
2.5 (3, 4) cm

4½"
11.5 cm

5¼ (5¾ 6¼)"
13.5 (14.5, 16) cm

12 (13¼, 14¼)"
30.5 (33.5, 36) cm

BACK

8¼ (8¾, 9¼)"
21 (22, 23.5) cm

21¼ (22¾, 24½)"
54.5 (57.5, 62.5) cm

10¾ (11¼, 12)"
27.5 (28.5, 30.5) cm

Gladys Fair Isle Bonnet

FAIR ISLE PROJECTS WERE EXTREMELY POPULAR IN BRITAIN DURING THE 1940S BECAUSE THEY CALLED FOR SMALL AMOUNTS OF WOOL IN MULTIPLE COLORS. THIS ALLOWED KNITTERS TO INCORPORATE LEFTOVER AND RECYCLED WOOL INTO THEIR PROJECTS DURING A TIME OF RATIONING AND SHORTAGES. BONNETS WERE POPULAR FOR DECADES BECAUSE MANY PEOPLE BELIEVED THEY WOULD PREVENT A BABY'S EARS FROM STICKING OUT LATER IN LIFE. THIS BRITISH WAR-ERA PATTERN IS KNIT IN TWO PIECES—A BAND THAT GOES AROUND THE FACE AND A BACK PANEL FOR THE BACK OF THE HEAD—THEN ASSEMBLED BEFORE A SEED-STITCH BORDER IS WORKED AROUND THE BOTTOM AND A SIMPLE EDGING IS CROCHETED AROUND THE FACE. THE PATTERN REQUIRES THAT YOU HANDLE THREE COLORS AT THE SAME TIME, SO IF YOU HAVEN'T DONE THAT BEFORE, PRACTICE ON A SWATCH UNTIL YOU GET THE HANG OF IT.

SIZES
12-18 months

FINISHED MEASUREMENTS
10½" (27 cm) wide at neck
8" (20.5 cm) high

YARN
Rowan Yarns 4-Ply Soft (100% Merino wool; 191 yards [175 meters] / 50 grams):
1 ball each #376 Nippy (MC), #387 Rain Cloud (A), and #396 Clover (B)

NEEDLES
One pair straight needles size US 2 (2.75 mm)
Change needle size if necessary to obtain correct gauge.

NOTIONS
Crochet hook size US C-2 (2.75 mm)

GAUGE
34 sts and 38 rows = 4" (10 cm) in Fair Isle pattern from Chart A

STITCH PATTERN

Seed Stitch (odd number of sts; 1-row repeat)
All Rows: *K1, p1; repeat from * to last st, k1.

BACK PANEL

Using MC, CO 13 sts. Begin Seed st. Work even for 4 rows.
Begin Fair Isle Pattern (RS): Begin Fair Isle pattern from Chart A. Work even until Chart A is complete, working increases and decreases as indicated in Chart. BO all sts.

FRONT PANEL

Using MC, CO 29 sts. Begin Seed st. Work even for 4 rows.
Begin Fair Isle Pattern (RS): Begin Fair Isle pattern from Chart B. Work even until 4 vertical repeats of Chart have been worked, then repeat Rows 1-20.
Next Row (RS): Change to Seed st. Work even for 4 rows. BO all sts.

FINISHING

Block pieces to measurements. With RS's facing, beginning at CO edges of Front Panel and Back Panel, sew right edge of Front Panel to left side, top, then right side of Back Panel. Press seam. With RS facing, using crochet hook and B, beginning at bottom right corner of Bonnet, work 2 rows single crochet along remaining side edge of Front Panel, then work 2 rows in MC, 2 rows in A, then 2 rows in MC. Fasten off. *Note: If you need a smaller or larger Bonnet, work fewer or more single crochet rows before fastening off.*

Ties: Cut two 2-yard (2-meter) long strands each of MC, A, and B. Holding 1 strand of each color together for each Tie, make 2 twisted cords 13" (33 cm) long as follows: Fold strands in half and secure one end to a stationary object. Twist from other end until cord begins to buckle. Fold twisted length in half and holding ends together, allow to twist up on itself. Tie cut end in an overhand knot to secure. Attach 1 Tie to each front corner. Trim ends even.

CHART A

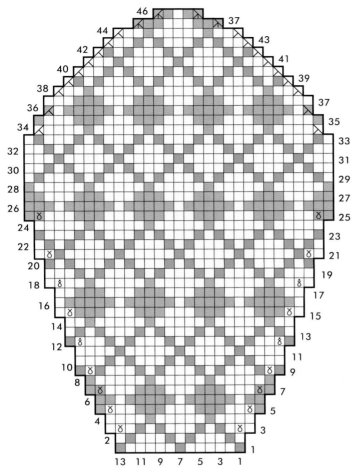

CHART B

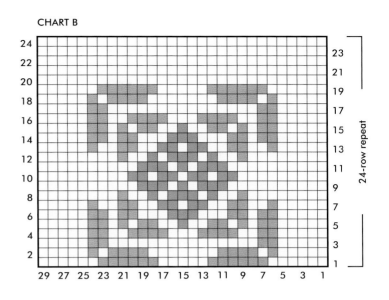

24-row repeat

KEY

☐ Knit on RS, purl on WS.

⌧ Make 1 knitwise

⌧ Make 1 purlwise

⬈ K2tog on RS, p2tog on WS.

⬊ Skp on RS, p2tog-tbl on WS.

⬈ K3tog

⬊ Sssk

☐ MC

▨ A

▨ B

Twyla Shoulderette

THIS GLAMOROUS LACE SHRUG FROM THE 1930S IS DECEPTIVELY SIMPLE TO MAKE.
YOU WORK A RECTANGLE IN THE FEATHER-AND-FAN STITCH, THEN SEW THE SIDES TOGETHER TO CREATE A
TUBE, LEAVING AN OPENING FOR BABY'S HEAD AND BACK AND LEAVING THE SHORT ENDS
OF THE TUBE OPEN TO FORM THE CUFFS. THIS PATTERN CAN BE ADJUSTED EASILY TO CUSTOM-FIT ANY SIZE
BABY – JUST CALCULATE BABY'S "WING SPAN" (THE MEASUREMENT FROM CUFF TO CUFF) AND KNIT
UNTIL YOU REACH THAT MEASUREMENT BEFORE STARTING THE SECOND CUFF.

SIZE
6-12 months (12-24 months)
Shown in size 6-12 months

FINISHED MEASUREMENTS
20 (21½)" [51 (55) cm] from cuff to cuff
5½ (6¾)" [14 (17) cm] from top to bottom,
after sewing seams

YARN
Louet Euroflax Sport Weight (100% wet
spun linen; 270 yards [247 meters] / 100
grams): 2 hanks #82 Great Lakes

NEEDLES
One pair straight needles size US 1
(2.25 mm)
One pair straight needles size US 3
(3.25 mm)
Change needle size if necessary to obtain
correct gauge.

NOTIONS
Crochet hook size US D-3 (3.25 mm);
1 yard (1 meter) ½" (1.5 cm) wide ribbon
(optional); sewing needle and thread
(optional)

GAUGE
24 sts and 28 rows = 4" (10 cm)
in Feather and Fan Pattern,
using larger needles

STITCH PATTERNS

2x2 Rib (multiple of 4 sts; 1-row repeat)
All Rows: *K2, p2; repeat from * to end.

Feather and Fan Pattern (multiple of 18 sts + 8; 4-row repeat) (see Chart)
Row 1 (RS): Knit.
Row 2: K4, purl to last 4 sts, k4.
Row 3: K4, *[k2tog] 3 times, [yo, k1] 6 times, [k2tog] 3 times; repeat from * to last 4 sts, k4.
Row 4: Knit.
Repeat Rows 1-4 for Feather and Fan Pattern.

SHOULDERETTE

Using smaller needles, CO 40 (48) sts. Begin 2x2 Rib. Work even for 1½" (4 cm), increase 0 (1) st on last row—40 (49) sts.
Increase Row (RS): Change to larger needles. *K1-f/b; repeat from * to end—80 (98) sts.
Begin Pattern (WS): Change to Feather and Fan Pattern (you may follow text or Chart for pattern), beginning with Row 2. Work even until piece measures 18½ (20)" [47 (51) cm] from the beginning, ending with Row 4 of pattern.
Decrease Row (RS): *Ssk, k2tog; repeat from * to end—40 (49) sts remain.
(WS) Change to smaller needles and 2x2 Rib decrease 0 (1) st on first row—40 (48) sts remain. Work even for 1½" (4 cm).

FINISHING

Sew side edges together for 4" (10 cm) from BO and CO edges; leave center 12 (13½)" [30.5 (34.5) cm] open. Using sewing needle and thread, sew ribbon to WS, along both edges of opening, for reinforcement (optional), being careful not to let sts show on RS.

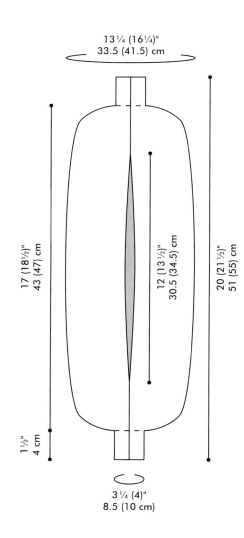

13 1/4 (16 1/4)"
33.5 (41.5) cm

17 (18 1/2)"
43 (47) cm

12 (13 1/2)"
30.5 (34.5) cm

20 (21 1/2)"
51 (55) cm

1 1/2"
4 cm

3 1/4 (4)"
8.5 (10 cm)

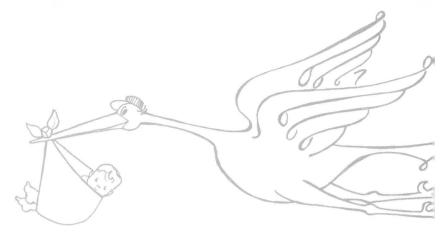

Making Gifts Special

Show your affection by knitting a project that suits baby as well as Mom and Dad.

Knit something detailed.

Most people, and especially non-knitters, respond to lace, cables, and intricate stitch patterns as if you just pulled a quarter out of their ear. If you don't have as much time as you'd like, keep it small (like booties or a hat)—but remember that success is all in the details.

Knit something soft.

There's a world of soft yarn out there, much of which can be machine-washed or quickly hand-washed. Pick a nice Merino or a washable blend that's so soft that Mom gasps when she pulls your present out of the box at the shower.

Choose practical or luxurious.

If baby's parents are practical types, knit something that they will turn to time and again, such as a garment that baby can wear day in and day out, like the Audrey Hoodie (page 22) or the Stella Pixie Hat (page 30). Or knit a pile of Frankie Socks (page 118) so high that Mom won't run out of socks for months. She may not think your gift is the lap of luxury when she opens the box, but she'll thank you all the more when it proves its usefulness later.

If Mom and Dad value luxury, choose a "high-profile" yarn for your gift, such as warm cashmere for the Billie Beret (page 16) or a soft angora blend for the Jackie Cabled Set (page 122).

KEY

☐   Knit on RS, purl on WS.

⊡   Purl on RS, knit on WS.

◯   Yo

◿   K2tog

FEATHER AND FAN PATTERN

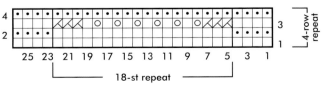

Oscar
Argyle Sweater

FROM A 1941 EDITION OF THE POPULAR *WOOLIES FOR BABIES* SERIES OF
PATTERN BOOKS, THIS THREE-COLOR ARGYLE STYLE WAS ALL THE RAGE IN THE 1940S AND EARLY 1950S.
THE ORIGINAL PATTERN CALLED FOR RED, YELLOW, AND BLUE YARN, BUT GIVEN THE EXPLOSION
OF OPTIONS AVAILABLE IN STORES AT THAT TIME, THE POSTWAR KNITTER WOULD HAVE EXPERIMENTED
WITH OTHER COLORS (AS I HAVE DONE HERE). WHILE THIS IS ONE OF THE MORE CHALLENGING PATTERNS
IN THIS BOOK, IT'S NOTHING YOU CAN'T TACKLE WITH A HEALTHY HELPING OF PATIENCE
AND A FEW GOOD TIPS. THE STRANDED COLORWORK REQUIRES THAT YOU HANDLE THREE COLORS AT
THE SAME TIME, REQUIRING "FLOATS" (OR LENGTHS OF YARN) TO BE CARRIED ALONG THE BACK SIDE
OF THE WORK. BE SURE TO WATCH YOUR TENSION SO THAT THE WORK DOESN'T PUCKER
AND SO THAT YOUR FLOATS AREN'T TOO LOOSE (IN WHICH CASE BABY COULD SNAG HIS OR HER FINGERS
ON THEM). THE BODY IS WORKED FLAT IN ONE PIECE, AND THEN THE SLEEVES ARE WORKED SEPARATELY.
TO MAKE THIS PROJECT FEEL MORE MANAGEABLE, CONSIDER KNITTING BOTH SLEEVES AT THE SAME TIME
ON ONE NEEDLE. YOU'LL SAVE YOURSELF SECOND-SLEEVE ENNUI AND THE TIME
YOU SPEND ON THE PROJECT WILL FLY BY.

SIZES
6-12 months (12-18 months,
18-24 months)
Shown in size 6-12 months

FINISHED MEASUREMENTS
20 ½ (23, 25 ½)" [52 (58, 65) cm] chest

YARN
RYC Cashsoft 4-Ply (57% extrafine Merino
wool / 33% microfiber / 10% cashmere;
197 yards [180 meters] / 50 grams): 2 (2,
3) balls #444 Amethyst (MC); 1 ball each
#435 Ginger (A) and #443 Kiwi (B)

NEEDLES
One pair straight needles
size US 2 (2.75 mm)
One pair straight needles
size US 3 (3.25 mm)
One set of five double-pointed
needles (dpn) size US 2 (2.75 mm)
Change needle size if necessary
to obtain correct gauge.

NOTIONS
Removable stitch markers

GAUGE
30 sts and 40 rows = 4" (10 cm) in
Stockinette stitch (St st), using larger needles
32 sts and 40 rows = 4" (10 cm) in Argyle
Pattern from Chart, using larger needles

STITCH PATTERN
1x1 Rib (multiple of 2 sts; 1-row/rnd repeat)
Row/Rnd 1 (RS): *K1, p1; repeat from * to end
[end k1 if an odd number of sts].
Row/Rnd 2: Knit the knit sts and purl the purl
sts as they face you.
Repeat Row/Rnd 2 for 1x1 Rib.

BACK
With smaller needles and MC, CO 81 (91, 101)
sts. Begin 1x1 Rib. Work even for 1½" (4 cm),
ending with a WS row.
Begin Chart (RS): Change to larger needles and
Argyle Pattern from Chart. Work even until
piece measures 8" (20.5 cm) from the beginning,
ending with a WS row.
Shape Armholes (RS): BO 3 sts at beginning of
next 2 rows, 2 sts at beginning of next 2 rows,
then decrease 1 st each side every other row
once—69 (79, 89) sts remain. Work even until
piece measures 3¾" (9.5 cm) from beginning of
armhole shaping, ending with Row 2 of Chart.
Next Row (RS): Change to MC. Work even until
armhole measures 4 (4¼, 4½)" [10 (11, 11.5) cm]
from beginning of shaping, ending with a WS
row. BO all sts. Place marker (pm) 15 (18, 21) sts
in from each edge, for shoulders.

KEY
☐ Knit on RS, purl on WS.
▨ MC
▨ A
▨ B

ARGYLE PATTERN

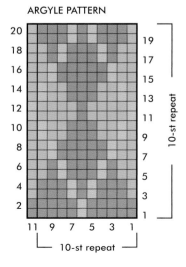

10-st repeat

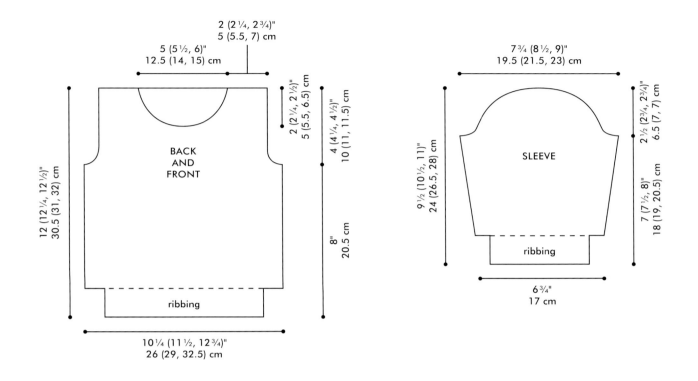

FRONT

Work as for Back until armhole measures 2"
(5 cm) from beginning of shaping, ending with a
WS row.

Shape Neck: Work 22 (26, 29) sts, join a second
ball of yarn, BO center 25 (27, 31) sts, work to
end. Working both sides at the same time, work
even for 1 row.

Next Row (RS): Decrease 1 st at each neck edge
this row, then every other row 6 (7, 7) times—15
(18, 21) sts remain each side for shoulders. Work
even until piece measures same as for Back to end
of Chart, ending with Row 2 of Chart.

Next Row (RS): Change to MC. Work even until
armhole measures 4 (4¼, 4½)" [10 (11, 11.5) cm]
from beginning of shaping, ending with a WS
row. BO all sts.

SLEEVES

With smaller needles and MC, CO 51 sts. Begin
1x1 Rib. Work even until piece measures 1½" (4
cm) from the beginning, ending with a WS row.

Next Row (RS): Change to larger needles and St
st. Work even for 2 rows.

Shape Sleeve (RS): Increase 1 st each side this
row, then every 16 (10, 8) rows 3 (5, 7) times—59
(63, 67) sts. Work even until piece measures 7
(7½, 8)" [18 (19, 20.5) cm] from the beginning,
ending with a WS row.

Shape Cap (RS): BO 3 sts at beginning of next
2 rows, decrease 1 st each side every other row
8 (8, 10) times, every 4 rows 1 (2, 1) time(s), then
BO 3 sts at beginning of next 2 rows—29 (31, 33)
sts remain. BO all sts.

FINISHING

Block pieces to measurements. Sew shoulder
seams. Set in Sleeves. Sew side and Sleeve seams.

Neckband: With RS facing, using dpns and MC,
and beginning at left shoulder seam, pick up
and knit 108 (120, 132) sts around neck shaping.
Join for working in the rnd; pm for beginning of
rnd. Begin 1x1 Rib. Work even for 12 rnds. BO
all sts in pattern. Fold Neckband to WS and sew
BO edge to pick-up edge.

Avery Christening Gown & Frock

IN THE LEAN YEARS FOLLOWING WORLD WAR II, WHEN THIS BRITISH PATTERN WAS FIRST PUBLISHED, SPENDING ANY MONEY AT ALL ON A GARMENT THAT WOULD ONLY BE WORN ONCE WAS AN EXTRAVAGANCE. STILL, THE LACY, OPEN STITCHWORK MADE IT COMPARATIVELY ECONOMICAL, REQUIRING LESS WOOL TO KNIT THAN A HEAVIER GARMENT OR ONE KNIT INTO A DENSER, LESS OPEN FABRIC. TWO STYLES WERE PRESENTED IN THE ORIGINAL PATTERN AND ARE GIVEN HERE. THE SHORTER ONE, WORKED IN SLIGHTLY HEAVIER YARN IN A LARGER GAUGE, MAKES A LOVELY PARTY FROCK FOR A YOUNG TODDLER.

SIZES
GOWN: 0-3 months
FROCK: 12-24 months

FINISHED MEASUREMENTS
GOWN: 18" (45.5 cm) chest
FROCK: 24" (61 cm) chest

YARN
GOWN: Jaggerspun Zephyr Wool-Silk (50% Merino wool / 50% Chinese Tussah silk; [4608 meters] / 1 lb [453 gram] cone): 3¾ ounces Vanilla
FROCK: Louet Gems Fingering Weight (100% Merino wool; 185 yards [169 meters] / 50 grams): 4 hanks #08 Lilac

NEEDLES
One pair straight needles size US 5 (3.75 mm)
One pair straight needles size US 3 (3.25 mm)
Change needle size if necessary to obtain correct gauge.

NOTIONS
Crochet hook size D-3 (3.25 mm) or size to match smaller needles; stitch marker; two ⁵⁄₁₆" (8 mm) buttons; 2 (1½) yards [2 (1.5) meters] ³⁄₈" (1 cm) wide ribbon

GAUGE
GOWN: 30 sts and 30 rows = 4" (10 cm) in Frost Flowers Pattern, using larger needles
24 sts and 36 rows = 4" (10 cm) in Openwork Pattern, using larger needles

FROCK: 26½ sts and 30 rows = 4" (10 cm) in Frost Flowers Pattern, using larger needles
20 sts and 36 rows = 4" (10 cm) in Openwork Pattern, using larger needles

NOTE
This pattern is for both the long Gown and a shorter Frock. The first set of figures is for the Gown; the second set of figures, shown in (), is for the Frock. Where only one set of figures is given, it applies to both Gown and Frock. When working shaping, if you cannot work a complete repeat after or before working the edge decreases, work sts in St st.

STITCH PATTERNS

Frost Flowers Pattern (multiple of 34 sts + 4; 24-row repeat) (see Chart)

Row 1 (RS): Slip 1, k1, *k3, k2tog, k4, yo, p2, [k2, yo, skp] 3 times, p2, yo, k4, skp, k3; repeat from * to last 2 sts, k2.

Row 2: Slip 1, k1, *p2, p2tog-tbl, p4, yo, p1, k2, [p2, yo, p2tog] 3 times, k2, p1, yo, p4, p2tog, p2; repeat from * to last 2 sts, k2.

Row 3: Slip 1, k1, *k1, k2tog, k4, yo, k2, p2, [k2, yo, skp] 3 times, p2, k2, yo, k4, skp, k1; repeat from * to last 2 sts, k2.

Row 4: Slip 1, k1, *p2tog-tbl, p4, yo, p3, k2, [p2, yo, p2tog] 3 times, k2, p3, yo, p4, p2tog; repeat from * to last 2 sts, k2.

Rows 5-12: Repeat Rows 1-4.

Row 13: Slip 1, k1, *yo, skp, k2, yo, skp, p2, yo, k4, skp, k6, k2tog, k4, yo, p2, k2, yo, skp, k2; repeat from * to last 2 sts, k2.

Row 14: Slip 1, k1, *yo, p2tog, p2, yo, p2tog, k2, p1, yo, p4, p2tog, p4, p2tog-tbl, p4, yo, p1, k2, p2, yo, p2tog, p2; repeat from * to last 2 sts, k2.

Row 15: Slip 1, k1, *yo, skp, k2, yo, skp, p2, k2, yo, k4, skp, k2, k2tog, k4, yo, k2, p2, k2, yo, skp, k2; repeat from * to last 2 sts, k2.

Row 16: Slip 1, k1, *yo, p2tog, p2, yo, p2tog, k2, p3, yo, p4, p2tog, p2tog-tbl, p4, yo, p3, k2, p2, yo, p2tog, p2; repeat from * to last 2 sts, k2.

Rows 17-24: Repeat Rows 13–16.

Repeat Rows 1-24 for Frost Flowers Pattern.

Openwork Pattern (multiple of 4 sts + 2; 2-row repeat) (see Chart)

Row 1: K1, *k2, yo, skp; repeat from * to last st, k1.

Row 2: K1, *p2, yo, p2tog; repeat from * to last st, k1.

Repeat Rows 1 and 2 for Openwork Pattern.

FRONT

With larger needles, CO 140 sts. Begin Garter st (knit every row). Work even for 6 rows.

Skirt

Begin Pattern (RS): Change to Frost Flowers Pattern (you may follow Chart or text for pattern). Work even until 7 (3) vertical repeats of Frost Flowers Pattern have been completed. Piece should measure 23 (10)" [58.5 (25.5) cm] from the beginning.

Shape Waist (RS): *K2tog; repeat from * to end—70 sts remain.

Eyelet Row: P1, *yo, p2tog; repeat from * to last st, p1.

KEY

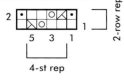

- ☐ Knit on RS, purl on WS.
- ⦁ Purl on RS, knit on WS.
- ☑ Slip st purlwise.
- ☉ Yo
- ◣ K2tog on RS, p2tog on WS.
- ◢ Skp on RS, p2tog-tbl on WS.

OPENWORK PATTERN

FROST FLOWERS PATTERN

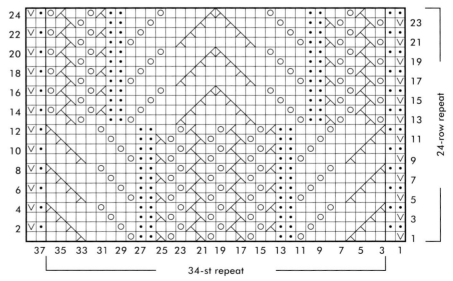

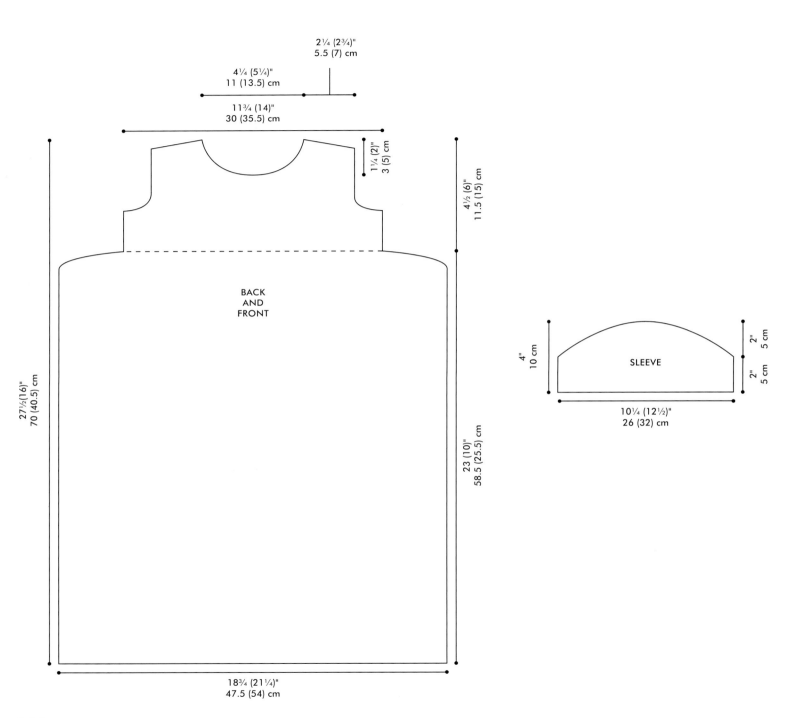

2¼ (2¾)"
5.5 (7) cm

4¼ (5¼)"
11 (13.5) cm

11¾ (14)"
30 (35.5) cm

1¼ (2)"
3 (5) cm

4½ (6)"
11.5 (15) cm

BACK
AND
FRONT

27½(16)"
70 (40.5) cm

23 (10)"
58.5 (25.5) cm

4"
10 cm

2"
5 cm

2"
5 cm

2"
5 cm

SLEEVE

10¼ (12½)"
26 (32) cm

18¾ (21¼)"
47.5 (54) cm

Yoke

Begin Pattern (RS): Change to smaller needles and Openwork Pattern (you may follow Chart or text for Pattern). Work even until piece measures 1" (2.5 cm) from beginning of Yoke, ending with a WS row.

Shape Armholes (RS): *Note: When working shaping, if you cannot work a complete repeat after or before working the edge decreases, work remaining repeat sts in St st.* BO 4 sts at beginning of next 2 rows, then 2 sts at beginning of next 4 rows—54 sts remain. Work even until Yoke measures 3¼ (4)" [8.5 (10) cm] from beginning of waist shaping, ending with a WS row.

Shape Neck (RS): Work 18 sts, join a second ball of yarn, BO center 18 sts, work to end. Working both sides at the same time, work even for 1 row.

Next Row (RS): BO 2 sts at each neck edge twice—14 sts remain each side for shoulders.

Shape Shoulders (RS): BO 7 sts at beginning of next 4 rows.

BACK

Work as for Front to beginning of Yoke. Place marker (pm) after st #37.

Yoke

Shape Back Neck Slit

Row 1 (RS): Change to smaller needles and Openwork Pattern, as follows: K1, *k2, yo, skp; repeat from * to 4 sts before marker, k4 (edge sts, keep in Garter st [knit every row]), remove marker; join a second ball of yarn, CO 4 sts for Button Band, *k2, yo, skp; repeat from * to last st, k1.

Row 2: Working both sides at the same time, on right side, k1, *p2, yo, p2tog; repeat from * to last 4 sts, k4 (edge sts, keep in Garter st); on left side, k4, *p2, yo, p2tog; repeat from * to last st, k1. Work even for 1", ending with a WS row.

Shape Armholes (RS): As for Front—29 sts remain each side.

Buttonhole Row (WS): On right side, work to end; on left side, k2, yo, k2tog, work to end. Work even until piece measures 3¼ (4)" [8.5 (10) cm] from beginning of waist shaping, ending with a RS row.

Next Row (WS): Repeat Buttonhole Row.

Shape Neck (RS): BO 11 sts at each neck edge once, then 2 sts twice—14 sts remain. Shape shoulders as for Back.

SLEEVES

With smaller needles, CO 48 sts. Begin Garter st. Work even for 2 rows.

Eyelet Row (RS): K1, *yo, k2tog; repeat from * to last st, k1.

Increase Row (WS): K4, [k1, m1, k2] 13 times, m1, k5—62 sts.

Begin Pattern (RS): Change to Openwork Pattern. Work even until piece measures 2" (5 cm) from the beginning, ending with a WS row.

Shape Cap (RS): BO 2 sts at beginning of next 16 rows—30 sts remain.

Next Row (RS): *K2tog; repeat from * to end—15 sts remain. BO all sts.

FINISHING

Block pieces to measurements. When blocking, stretch Skirt firmly to shape lace pattern but do not stretch Yoke or Sleeves. Sew shoulder seams. Set in Sleeves. Sew side and Sleeve seams.

Neck Edging: With RS facing, using crochet hook, beginning at top of Back neck slit, work edging around neck shaping as follows:

Row 1: Work 1 double crochet (dc) in first st, *ch3, skip next 3 sts, work 1 dc in next st; repeat from * to end. Turn work.

Row 2: Ch1, work 1 single crochet (sc) in space created by ch3 of Row 1, ch4, work 1 sc in same space, *sc in next space, ch4, sc in same space; repeat from * to end. Sew CO sts of Button Band to WS of top of Skirt, being careful not to let sts show on RS. Sew buttons to Button Band, opposite buttonholes. Thread ribbon through Eyelet Rows on Skirt; tie in bow.

Frances Nursing Shawl

THIS SOFT, SPRINGY SHAWL FROM A 1945 BABY BOOK IS GENEROUSLY SIZED FOR
PRIVACY WHEN NURSING – AND IT CAN DOUBLE AS A LIGHTWEIGHT BLANKET
ON A SPRING DAY. THE ORIGINAL PATTERN CALLED FOR A GARTER-STITCH CENTER, BUT I'VE
ADDED A SIMPLE KNIT-PURL PATTERN IN THE CENTER TO USE LESS YARN. THE LACE
PANELS ARE WORKED SEPARATELY AND THEN SEWN ON.

FINISHED MEASUREMENTS
47" x 47" (119.5 x 119.5 cm), after blocking

YARN
Blue Moon Fiber Arts Socks that Rock
Lightweight (100% superwash Merino wool;
360 yards [329 meters] / 128 grams):
7 hanks Hoofle Poofle

NEEDLES
One 32" (80 cm) circular (circ)
needle size US 5 (3.75 mm)
Change needle size if necessary
to obtain correct gauge.

GAUGE
22 sts and 40 rows = 4" (10 cm)
in Ridge Pattern
28 sts and 32 rows = 4" (10 cm)
in Lace Pattern

KEY

☐	Knit on RS, purl on WS.
⊡	Purl on RS, knit on WS.
⊙	Yo
◹	K2tog on RS, p2tog on WS.
⊠	P2tog on RS
◺	Sk2p on WS
◿	K3tog on RS
▨	No stitch

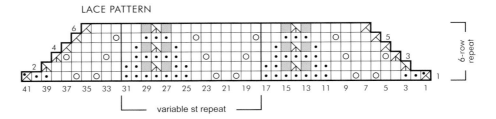

LACE PATTERN

NOTE: The decreases at each edge will shift the pattern 7 sts toward the center with every 6-row repeat, which will cause the main pattern repeat to offset by 7 sts.

STITCH PATTERNS

Ridge Pattern (any number of sts; 4-row repeat)
Rows 1 and 3 (RS): Knit.
Row 2: Purl.
Row 4: Knit.
Repeat Rows 1-4 for Ridge Pattern.

Lace Pattern (multiple varies; 6-row repeat)
(see Chart)
Note: St count changes from row to row as increases and decreases are worked.
Row 1 (RS): P2tog, p2, *k2, yo, k1, yo, k2, p7; repeat from * to last 9 sts, end k2, yo, k1, yo, k2, p2, p2tog.
Row 2: Sk2p, p7, *k2, sk2p, k2, p7; repeat from * to last 3 sts, sk2p.

Row 3: K3tog, yo, k3, yo, k2, p5, k1, *k1, yo, k3, yo, k2, p5, k1; repeat from * to last 8 sts, k1, yo, k3, yo, k1, k3tog.
Row 4: P2tog, p5, *p1, k1, sk2p, k1, p8; repeat from * to last 14 sts, p1, k1, sk2p, k1, p6, p2tog.
Row 5: K2tog, k3, yo, k2, p3, k2, *yo, k5, yo, k2, p3, k2; repeat from * to last 5 sts, yo, k3, k2tog.
Row 6: P2tog, p3, *p2, sk2p, p9; repeat from * to last 12 sts, p2, sk2p, p5, p2tog.

CENTER PANEL
CO 181 sts. Begin Ridge Pattern. Work even until piece measures 30" from the beginning, ending with a WS row. BO all sts.

SIDE PANELS (make 4)
CO 289 sts. Knit 1 row. Begin Lace Pattern (you may follow text or Chart for pattern). Work even for 54 rows (9 vertical pattern repeats), working decreases as indicated in Chart or text. BO all sts LOOSELY. *Note: Since this piece will be blocked larger than when it comes off the needles, you may wish to BO with a needle one size larger than working needles to ensure that BO edge is elastic.*

FINISHING
Block Center Panel to 34" x 34" (86 x 86 cm). Block Side Panels so that BO edge is 34" (86 cm) wide and CO edge is 47" (119.5 cm) wide. Sew BO edges of Side Panels to sides of Center Panel. Sew side edges of Side Panels together.

CHAPTER THREE

DIY VINTAGE:
FINDING AND EVALUATING
VINTAGE PATTERNS

If you would like to begin your own collection of vintage patterns, here are some tips on where to look and what to look for:

First, you need a source. If you're not the type to spend hours upending musty boxes in church rummage bins and at estate sales, don't despair—online auction sites like eBay present a great opportunity to stock up, though patterns from these sources often cost more than patterns unearthed at "real-world" sales. Used booksellers are another resource; they tend to list what they have in stock in the knitting and sewing sections of their online stores.

Many blogs and free pattern websites offer patterns that have passed into the public domain free of charge. A few commercial websites also offer reproductions of copyright-free vintage patterns, originally published between the 1800s and the 1950s, at reasonable prices.

If you are ordering a pattern online, you may only see a picture of the design and may not have an opportunity to read through it before you buy. If you do find a vintage pattern that you have an opportunity to examine before buying, consider it the same way you would a modern pattern. Is it complete? How detailed are the instructions? Does it include charts or (more rarely) schematics? In the photograph, is the model positioned so that you can see if the garment hangs properly? Since most vintage patterns don't include schematics, try to find ones that show the garment flat, so you can tell what you're getting into and get a good sense of what the garment should look like knitted up. Double-check the needle requirements to make sure you know what they mean. Check the needle size against the recommended gauge for the pattern, keeping in mind the thickness of fabric required (for example, if it is supposed to be a dense pattern worked on small needles, or a lacy one worked on large needles). The charts at right will help you to convert knitting needle and crochet hook sizes, if necessary.

KNITTING NEEDLE CONVERSION CHART

Needle sizes in vintage patterns varied by type of needle and by their country of origin. American needles were sized differently than British needles, and vintage British sizes also differed from the metric sizing used there and in most European countries today. When knitting from an original vintage pattern, use this chart to determine what modern-size needle applies.

METRIC SIZE	US Size	UK Size	Steel DPNs
2 mm	0	14	13
2.25 mm	1	13	12
2.5 mm	1.5	-	-
2.75 mm	2	12	11
3 mm	2.5	11	10
3.25 mm	3	10	-
3.5 mm	4	-	9
3.75 mm	5	9	8
4 mm	6	-	-
4.5 mm	7	7	-
5 mm	8	6	-
5.5 mm	9	5	-
6 mm	10	4	-
6.5 mm	10.5	3	-
7 mm	-	2	-
7.5 mm	-	1	-
8 mm	11	0	-
9 mm	13	00	-
10 mm	15	000	-

CHOOSING YARNS FOR VINTAGE PATTERNS

To help you choose yarns for vintage patterns that you might want to follow, here are a few tips to keep in mind.

Be aware of weight changes. In my work with patterns of the 1920s through the 1950s, I have noticed a significant change in yarn weights. For example, many of the yarns called for in these patterns—particularly those for baby—were made using a different spinning process than is used today. Yarn today seems to be denser per yard than it was 75 years ago. Three ounces of the less densely spun, airier wool of 1930 might have the same yardage and thickness as six or seven ounces of modern, more densely spun yarn. For this reason, weight is not the best indicator of how much yarn you will need. This presents a challenge, as almost all vintage patterns list yarn requirements by weight only—but by following a few easy steps you can deduce how much yarn you will need.

Look at the gauge required for the project. If you know you are looking at a project that calls for 8 stitches to the inch, you can make a pretty safe bet that you can use another yarn that, according to its ball band, knits up at 8 stitches to the inch. Keep in mind what the fabric is probably supposed to look like when assessing the proper gauge. Consider if the garment is meant to be loose and open (as it would generally be with lace) or tight and dense (as it might be with a toy or an outdoor jacket.)

Look at total yardage needed in addition to weight. If yardage requirements are given, you have a rough idea of how much yarn you will need already. Choose a yarn with a similar recommended gauge, and swatch to make sure that it looks good knitted up and that it looks like the fabric shown in the pattern photo. If the pattern does not list the yardage, try searching for it on the list of discontinued yarns at **http://www.vintageknits.com**. This site contains a database that lists weight and yardage information for many vintage yarns.

CROCHET HOOK CONVERSION CHART

When working from a vintage pattern, use this chart to decide what size hook applies. If the pattern does not specify a hook size, choose a hook with a comparable metric size to the knitting needles specified for the project.

METRIC SIZE	US Size	UK Size
2 mm	-	14
2.25 mm	B-1	13
2.5 mm	-	12
2.75 mm	C-2	-
3 mm	-	11
3.25 mm	D-3	10
3.5 mm	E-4	9
3.75 mm	F-5	-
4 mm	G-6	8
4.5 mm	7	7
5 mm	H-8	6
5.5 mm	I-9	5
6 mm	J-10	4
6.5 mm	K-10½	3
7 mm	-	2
8 mm	L-11	0
9 mm	M/N-13	00
10 mm	N/P-15	000

Vintage Knitting Tools

Every knitter has spotted them: coffee cans of colorful aluminum needles sitting forlornly in the thrift store or on the rummage sale bargain table. Well, the next time you see them, grab them, because those old needles are still good! For the most part, sizing hasn't changed a bit, so a size 10 from 1944 is still a size 10 today. (There used to be a different sizing system for double-pointed needles in the United States, but today they are sized the same as their single-pointed counterparts.) Even British needles, which were once sized using a different convention, are still useable once you measure them. (To make sure you have the right size, check all needles with a needle gauge and mark any differences with a piece of tape.) On page 150 is a conversion chart for British, metric, and American needle sizes.

If you're lucky enough to find them, needles made of bakelite, celluloid, and faux tortoiseshell are highly collectible. Vintage ivory needles, however, are best left alone. Because it is difficult to tell the difference between old and new ivory and poachers frequently pass off their wares as "antique," the sale of vintage ivory is highly restricted.

Other notions that you might enjoy collecting are old needle gauges, tape measures, embroidery scissors (especially the ones that look like storks and herons), needle cases, and bags.

If you still can't find the information on yardage, don't despair. You will just need to do some estimating. By using the gauge measurements given in the pattern, you can work out an idea of how many square inches the garment will be by multiplying its length and width. Even if measurements are not given for the finished piece, you can figure out a rough estimate of the square inches of knitting by multiplying the gauge by the number of stitches at the widest point of the garment. For instance, if the back of a baby cardigan is knit at 6 stitches per inch (2.5 cm), and the back is 60 stitches across at its widest point and the pattern is worked for a total of 10" (25.5 cm), then 60/6 = 10" (25.5 cm) wide x 10" (25.5 cm) long = 100" (254 cm) square.

Next, make a swatch in the yarn you intend to use, at the gauge required in the main stitch pattern. Your swatch should be at least 4" (10 cm) by 4" (10 cm). Weigh this swatch on a gram scale. If you know that your chosen yarn has 200 yards (183 meters) to 50 grams, and your swatch weighs 10 grams, then you know that 200 yards (183 meters) equal 50 grams, and 4 yards (3.5 meters) equal 1 gram. You can then conclude that your 10 gram swatch was made with approximately 40 yards (36.5 meters).

Now measure your swatch and multiply its length in inches by its width in inches. For example, if you made a 4" (10 cm) x 4" (10 cm) swatch, your swatch would be 16" (100 cm) square. If your swatch required 40 yards (36.5 meters), then you know that you will require roughly 2½ yards (2.5 meters) per square inch. Let's say that the back of your baby cardigan would measure 100" (254 cm) square, and that the fronts and sleeves each would measure 60" (152.5 cm) square, for a total of 340" (863.5 cm) square. At 2½ yards (2.5 meters) per square inch, the sweater will require roughly 850 yards (777 meters) of your chosen yarn.

This method is only a rough estimate. To be on the safe side, whatever your final calculation, be sure to get about 10-20% more yarn. Many yarn stores will allow you to return or exchange unused yarn as long as it is still in the skein and has not been over-fondled.

Consider the weight of the yarn originally called for. While the weight given in the pattern may not be the best indicator of the quantity of yarn you will need today, it is still relevant information when figuring out how to achieve comparable results. For example, if you substitute heavy cotton for light wool, you might end up with a heavy, droopy sweater. Or, if you are choosing a lightweight cabled yarn to substitute for a denser worsted-spun yarn of similar yardage, your garment may not have the substance and structure that the designer originally intended.

Consider the texture of the yarn. Study the photograph to see what kind of information you can gather. For example, try to determine if the yarn shown is shiny or fleecy, tightly or softly spun. To help you further, below is a list of vintage yarn types that you might encounter in a vintage knitting pattern.

- **Fingering yarn** in vintage patterns is similar to a fingering-weight yarn today; it came in 2-, 3- and 4-ply. The higher quality fingering yarns generally had more plies and therefore tended to be somewhat more durable. Fingering was the most commonly used yarn of the 1930s through the 1950s.
- **Germantown** or **Zephyr** was a soft, smooth-textured yarn that would have been used for afghans and baby garments, usually in a sport weight.
- **Jiffy yarn** or **quick-knitting** yarn was considered to be a very thick and bulky wool, but it varied greatly from company to company, with some companies marketing double-knitting weight yarn as "Jiffy" and others marketing yarn that would today be considered a super-bulky yarn.
- **Knitting worsted** would actually have been a double-knitting or light worsted-weight yarn today. It was usually made of rougher wool than would be used for next-to-the-skin wear, and was reserved for outerwear or hard-wearing soldiers' garments.
- **Lady Betty** was a soft, fleecy yarn meant for baby garments and lingerie; it only came in pastel colors as a 2-ply or 3-ply fingering weight yarn.
- **Saxony** was a fine 2-ply, 3-ply or 4-ply yarn usually used for baby garments.
- **Shetland Floss** was a fine, loosely spun, 2-ply yarn with a somewhat hairy texture, used for lace knitting such as shawls.
- **Soft knitting** was a soft but tightly twisted fingering weight yarn, used primarily for socks. Indeed, the closest thing to it today would be a high-quality Merino sock yarn.
- **Vest wool** was an early form of washable wool, guaranteed to be preshrunk.

INFANT MEASUREMENTS

This chart provides average baby measurements (not clothing sizes). Of course, some babies may be larger or smaller. Be sure to add 2 to 4" ease (or extra room for the baby to fit into) to these measurements when determining the size garment to make.

MEASUREMENT	0-3 months	3-6 months	6-12 months	12-18 months	18-24 months
Head Circumference	15"	16"	17"	18"	19"
Approx. Height	22-25"	26-30"	31-33"	32-34"	32-36"
Approx. Weight (lbs)	5-10	8-12	12-18	19-24	22-28
Chest Size	17"	18"	19"	20"	21"
Sleeve Length to Underarm	6"	6½"	7"	7½"	8"
Hips (includes diapers)	19"	20"	21"	22"	23"
Rise (measurement from waist to back of waist through legs)	12½"	14"	16"	18"	20"
Inseam (inner thigh to ankle)	6"	7½"	8½"	10½"	12½"
Foot length (toe to heel)	3¾"	4¼"	4½"	4¾"	5¼"

RECOMMENDED READING

1940s Knitting Books

In the 1940s, a number of classic texts on the subject of knitting were published. Unlike typical throwaway pattern books, which focused on the fashion of the day, these hardcover books sought to provide the knitter with all the knowledge she would need to create garments for an entire household. Part instruction manual, part stitch dictionary, part pattern book, they gave sage advice on everything from how to buy yarn and supplies to how to perform any knitting technique. The patterns offer a wonderful window into men's, women's, and children's clothing of the period. The technique sections and advice are still surprisingly relevant today, and are among the books I turn to repeatedly. Should you happen upon one of these books, I encourage you to buy it.

The Baby Book of Knitting and Crochet, Elizabeth Laird Mathieson, 1948, Spool Cotton Company, New York.
This all-baby book includes numerous designs from the popular "Woolies for Babies" pattern line, as well as advice on everything from tools to yarn to knitting and finishing. It features many charming baby projects, including some of the cutest crocheted and knitted toys I have ever seen.

The Complete Guide to Modern Knitting and Crocheting, Alice Carroll, 1947, Wm. H. Wise & Co., New York.
Perhaps the best of all the great knitting books of the 1940s, this comprehensive guide was written by one of the few doyennes of knitting whose fame allowed her to be credited for her work. This book is not only useful and wise but a joy to read. It includes an easy-to-understand explanation of the principles of dressmaking as they apply to everyday knitting—an innovative and rewarding approach to knitting. With over forty gorgeous vintage patterns for everything from men's and women's clothing to baby's and children's things to items for the home.

Complete Home Knitting Illustrated and *Practical Knitting*, Margaret Murray and Jane Koster, date unknown, Odhams Press Limited, London.
These two excellent books offer wise instruction as well as a glimpse into postwar knitting in Europe. Murray and Koster were two of the premier knitting-book authors of their time and among the few designers whose works were credited to them by the publishers. Their reputation was well deserved as the books themselves are gorgeously written and full of useful information.

Knitting History

Knitting America: A Glorious Heritage from Warm Socks to High Art, Susan M. Strawn, 2007, Voyageur Press, Minnesota.
This marvelous book tells the story of knitting in the United States from colonial times to the present. Packed with fascinating information as well as with hundreds of photos of knitters, garments, advertisements, and magazine covers, it also includes twenty historical knitting patterns that span American knitting history.

No Idle Hands: The Social History of American Knitting, Anne L. Macdonald, 1990, Ballantine Books, New York.
Through excerpts taken from diaries, letters, and other firsthand accounts, this book offers a fascinating documentation of the importance of knitting in the United States, from the earliest settlers to the modern age.

VINTAGE PATTERN SOURCES

Retroknit Design www.retroknit.net
Vintage patterns as well as the author's original designs.

Iva Rose Vintage Reproductions www.ivarose.com
Vast collection of copyright-free reproduction vintage pattern books for sale, with hundreds of titles first published from the 1800s to the 1930s.

Vintage Knits www.vintageknits.com
Original twentieth-century knitting, crochet, and needlework patterns at very reasonable prices.

Yesterknits www.yesterknits.com
Advertises the largest collection of vintage patterns in the world, with over 250,000 individual designs.

Vintage Purls www.vintagepurls.net.nz
Plenty of beautiful patterns that have passed into the public domain.

1940s Patterns to Knit – The Victoria & Albert Museum
www.vam.ac.uk/collections/fashion/features/knitting/1940s/index.html
Part of the Victoria & Albert Museum's excellent resource on knitting during the 1940s, this site features numerous free vintage patterns, including one for a darling knitted tiger toy.

YARN SOURCES

Following is contact information for the companies that produce and/or distribute the yarns used in the projects in this book. Contact them if your favorite yarn retailers cannot provide you with what you need.

Artyarns
914-428-0333
www.artyarns.com

Blue Moon Fiber Arts
866-802-9687
www.bluemoonfiberarts.com

Blue Sky Alpacas
888-460-8862
www.blueskyalpacas.com

Cascade Yarns
www.cascadeyarns.com

Cherry Tree Hill Yarns
802-525-3311
www.cherryyarn.com

Dale of Norway
802-383-0132
www.daleofnorway.com

Fleece Artist
www.fleeceartist.com

Frog Tree Yarns
T & C Imports
508-385-8862
www.frogtreeyarns.com

Hand Jive
916-806-8063
www.handjiveknits.com

Jaggerspun Yarn
www.jaggeryarn.com

Lorna's Laces
773-935-3803
www.lornaslaces.net

Louet North America
800-897-6444
www.louet.com

Mission Falls
877-244-1204
www.missionfalls.com

Pear Tree Yarn Australia
Jumbuk Fibre
www.peartreeyarn.com

Rowan & RYC
Westminster Fibers
800-445-9276
www.knitrowan.com

Sheep Shop
401-398-7656
www.sheepshopyarn.com

Sirdar Knitting Fever Inc.
516-546-3600
www.knittingfever.com

VT Organic Fiber Company
802-388-1313
www.o-wool.com

NOTIONS SOURCES

Eucalan
(fine wool wash with lanolin)
800-561-9731
www.eucalan.co

Hanah Silk Hand-Dyed Ribbons
(ribbons)
888-233-5187
www.artemisinc.com

M&J Trimming
(buttons, ribbons, trims, supplies)
800-965-8746
www.mjtrim.com

Purl and Purl Patchwork
(fabric, ribbons, yarns, supplies)
800-597-7875
www.purlsoho.com

Repro Depot
(ribbons, fabric, supplies)
413-527-4047
www.reprodepot.com

Soak Wash Inc.
(fine garment wash)
905-270-7625
www.soakwash.com

Tender Buttons
(vintage buttons)
143 East 62nd Street
New York, NY 10065
212-758-7004

PROP AND WARDROBE SOURCES

Flora and Henri
206-749-0004
www.florahenri.com

Mill Valley Baby and Kids Company
415-389-1312
www.mvbabyandkids.com

Mill Valley Mercantile
415-388-9588
www.millvalleyshop.com

PATTERN BIBLIOGRAPHY

Archie Vest
"722," *Dritz Baby Book Volume 8, 1947*, John Dritz & Sons, USA, page 27.

Audrey Hoodie
"Knitted Hood Sacque," *Columbia-Minerva Quick-Knit Baby Book Volume 78, 1957*, Columbia-Minerva Corporation, USA, page 3.

Avery Christening Gown & Frock
"Christening Robe," *Stitchcraft Babies Book, 1940s*, Stitchcraft Company, Great Britain, page 10.

Betty Lou Lace Cardigan
"Betty Lou #414," *Columbia Baby Book Volume 104, 1944*, James Lees & Sons Company, USA, page 14.

Billie Beret
"Baby Boy's Sweater and Beret," *Columbia Hand Knits for Infants and Children Volume 79, 1936*, Wm. H. Horstmann Company, USA, page 26.

Bobby Kimono
"Mimosa #410," *Columbia Baby Book Volume 104, 1944*, James Lees and Sons Company, USA, page 10.

Bunny Blanket
"Blanket no. 689," *Hand Knits by Beehive for Babies Volume 120-A, 1946*, Patons & Baldwins, Inc., USA, page 43.

Cleo Kitty Slippers
"Pussy Cat Slippers," *Paragon Baby Book No.10*, Paragon Alliance Ltd., New Zealand, page 7.

Daisy Soakers
"Pilch," *The French Baby Book, Weldon's Practical Knitting No. 380, 1940s*, The Amalgamated Press Ltd., Great Britain, page 20.

Dewey Cabled Pullover
"Frolic Cabled Slipover," *The Baby Book of Bear Brand – Bucilla Yarns Volume 319, 1941*, Bernhard Ullmann Company, USA, page 13.

Ducky Onesie
"Chick-A-Dee #3166," *Fleisher Fashions for Babies up to 4 Volume 75, 1940s*, Fleisher Yarns, Inc., USA, page 34.

Elmer the Elephant
"Toy Elephant," *The First Twelve Months, 1950s*, Patons & Baldwins Ltd., Australia, page 29.

Felix Cardigan & Pants Set
"Prince Pussycat Set," *Spinnerin #123, 1954*, Spinnerin Yarn Co., USA, page 27.

Floyd Pullover
"Columbia Slipover no. 5092," *Columbia Yarns Infants' and Children's Wear Manual of Knitting and Crocheting, 1929*, Wm. H. Horstmann Company, USA, page 37.

Frances Nursing Shawl
"#5295," *Woolies for Babies Book No. 224 2nd Edition, 1945*, Spool Cotton Company, USA, page 7.

Frankie Striped Socks
"Sock and Mitten Set," *Star Baby Book No. 96, 1953*, American Thread Company, USA, page 19.

Gladys Fair Isle Bonnet
"Fair Isle Bonnet & Mittens," Bestway Pattern #1708, 1940s, The Amalgamated Press Ltd., Great Britain.

Harry Sailor Sweater
"#370 Jack Tar Fashions," *Hand Knits by Beehive for Babies Volume 120-A, 1946*, Patons & Baldwins, Inc., USA, page 28.

Hazel Cape
"Cozy Travellers," *The First Twelve Months, 1950s*, Patons & Baldwins, Ltd., Australia, page 18.

Horace the Horse
"Horace #5343," *Minerva Baby and Juvenile Book Volume 53, 1939*, James Lees & Sons Company, USA, page 43.

Jackie Cabled Set
"Baby's Six Piece Knitted Set," *Jack Frost Baby Book Volume 60,* 1959, Gottlieb Bros., USA, page 8.

Jasper Diamond Hoodie
"Hooded Jacket Set #2155," *Bear Brand Baby Book Infants to 4 Years Volume 229,* 1950, Bernhard Ullmann Company, USA, page 11.

Liza Sideways Sacque
"Infant's Sacque #2813", *Columbia Yarn Book of Infant's Wear,* 1924, Wm. H. Horstmann Company, USA, page 23.

Louise Cardigan
"Buzzy Bee," *Patons Knitting Book #544,* 1940s, Patons & Baldwins Ltd., Australia, page 10.

Maude Honeycomb Blanket
"First Outing #3157," *Fleisher Fashions for Babies up to 4 Volume 75,* 1940s, Fleisher Yarns, Inc., USA, p.10.

Milo Soakers
"No. 5252," *Woolies for Babies Book No. 197,* 1943, Spool Cotton Company, USA, page 7.

Monty Snowsuit with Cap & Mittens
"Two Piece Snowsuit with Cap & Mittens," *Nomotta Baby Book,* 1959, Pauline Denham Yarns, Inc., USA, page 30.

Oscar Argyle Sweater
"Argyle Pullover #5151," *Woolies for Babies Volume 178,* 1942, Spool Cotton Company, USA, page 4.

Otto Short-Sleeved Pullover
"723," *Dritz Baby Book Volume 8,* 1947, John Dritz & Sons, USA, page 27.

Pearl Shrug
"In Good Humour Baby's Jacket," *Designs for Restful Living by Beehive, Series No. 49,* 1940s, Patons & Baldwins Ltd., Canada, page 15.

Rufus Textured Cardigan
"Mischievous One," *Paragon Baby Book No. 8,* 1950s, Paragon Art Needlecraft Ltd., New Zealand, page 2.

Rupert the Lion
"Rupert," *Weldon's Knitting Series No. 4,* late 1920s, Weldon's Publishing Company, Great Britain, page 2.

Stella Pixie Hat
"Red Riding Hood no. 1889," *Bear Brand – Bucilla Baby Book Volume 328,* 1944, Bernhard Ullmann Company, USA, page 23.

Twyla Shoulderette
"Shoulderette in the Feather & Fan Stitch #4135," *Minerva Juvenile and Baby Book Volume 41,* 1935, James Lees & Sons Company, USA, page 48.

Violet Sacque
"Sacque and Cap," *Fleisher's Baby Book for Infants to 4 Years, Volume 101,* 1947, Fleisher Yarns Inc., USA, page 8.

Abbreviations

BO Bind off
Ch Chain
Circ Circular
CO Cast on
Dc (double crochet) Working from right to left, yarn over hook (2 loops on hook), insert hook into the next stitch, yarn over hook and pull up a loop (3 loops on hook), [yarn over and draw thorough 2 loops] twice.
Dpn Double-pointed needle(s) loops on hook), yarn over and draw through all 3 loops on hook.
K Knit
K2tog Knit 2 sts together.
K3tog Knit 3 sts together.
K1-f/b Knit into front loop and back loop of same stitch to increase one stitch.
M1 With the tip of the left-hand needle inserted from front to back, lift the strand between the two needles onto the left-hand needle; knit the strand through the back loop to increase one stitch.
P Purl
P2tog Purl 2 sts together.
Pm Place marker
Psso (pass slipped stitch over) Pass slipped st on right-hand needle over the sts indicated in the instructions, as in binding off.
Rnd round
RS Right side

Sc (single crochet) Insert hook into next st and draw up a loop (2 loops on hook), yarn over and draw through both loops on hook.
Skp (slip, knit, pass) Slip next st knitwise to right-hand needle, k1, pass slipped st over knit st.
Sm Slip marker
Ssk (slip, slip, knit) Slip the next 2 sts to the right-hand needle one at a time as if to knit; return them back to left-hand needle one at a time in their new orientation; knit them together through the back loop(s).
Sssk (slip, slip, slip, knit) Same as ssk, but worked on next 3 sts.
Ssp (slip, slip, purl) Slip the next 2 sts to right-hand needle one at a time as if to knit; return them to the left-hand needle one at a time in their new orientation; purl them together through the back loop(s).
St(s) stitch(es)
K1-tbl Knit one stitch through the back loop, twisting the stitch.
Tbl Through the back loop
Tog Together
WS Wrong side
Wrp-t Wrap and turn (see Special Techniques-Short Row Shaping)
Wyib With yarn in back
Wyif With yarn in front
Yo Yarnover

Special Techniques

Cable CO: Make a loop (using a slip knot) with the working yarn and place it on the left-hand needle [first st CO], knit into slip knot, draw up a loop but do not drop st from left-hand needle; place new loop on left-hand needle; *insert the tip of the right-hand needle into the space between the last 2 sts on the left-hand needle and draw up a loop; place the loop on the left-hand needle. Repeat from * for remaining sts to be CO, or for casting on at the end of a row in progress.

Crochet Chain: Make a slip knot and place it on crochet hook. Holding tail end of yarn in left hand, *take hook under ball end of yarn from front to back; draw yarn on hook back through previous st on hook to form new st. Repeat from * to desired number of sts or length of chain.

Fringe: Using number of strands required in pattern, fold in half; with RS of piece facing, insert crochet hook just above edge to receive fringe, from back to front; catch the folded strands of yarn with the hook and pull through work to form a loop, insert ends of yarn through loop and pull to tighten.

Kitchener Stitch: Using a blunt yarn needle, thread a length of yarn approximately 4 times the length of the section to be joined. Hold the pieces to be joined wrong sides together, with the needles holding the sts parallel, both ends pointing to the right. Working from right to left, insert yarn needle into first st on front needle as if to purl, pull yarn through, leaving st on needle; insert yarn needle into first st on back needle as if to knit, pull yarn through, leaving st on needle; *insert yarn needle into first st on front needle as if to knit, pull yarn through, remove st from needle; insert yarn needle into next st on front needle as if to purl, pull yarn through, leave st on needle; insert yarn needle into first st on back needle as if to purl, pull yarn through, remove st from needle; insert yarn needle into next st on back needle as if to knit, pull yarn through, leave st on needle. Repeat from *, working 3 or 4 sts at a time, then go back and adjust tension to match the pieces being joined. When 1 st remains on each needle, cut yarn and pass through last 2 sts to fasten off.

Pompom: You can use a pompom maker or the following method: Cut two cardboard circles in the diameter of the pompom desired. Cut a ½" diameter hole in the center of each circle. Cut away a small wedge out of each circle to allow for wrapping yarn. Hold the circles together with the openings aligned. Wrap yarn around the circles until there is no room left in the center to wrap. Carefully cut yarn around outer edge of the cardboard circles. Using a 12" length of yarn, wrap around strands between the two circles and tie tightly. Slip the cardboard circles off the completed pompom; trim pompom, leaving the ends of the tie untrimmed. Using ends of tie, sew pompom to garment.

Short Row Shaping: Work the number of sts specified in the instructions, wrap and turn [wrp-t] as follows: Bring yarn to the front (purl position), slip the next st to the right-hand needle, bring yarn to back of work, return slipped st on right-hand needle to left-hand needle; turn, ready to work the next row, leaving remaining sts unworked.

When Short rows are completed, or when working progressively longer Short Rows, work the wrap together with the wrapped st as you come to it as follows: If st is to be worked as a knit st, insert the right-hand needle into the wrap, from below, then into the wrapped st; k2tog; if st to be worked is a purl st, insert needle into the wrapped st, then down into the wrap; p2tog. (Wrap may be lifted onto the left-hand needle, then worked together with the wrapped st if this is easier.)

Acknowledgments

Creating *Vintage Baby Knits* was a journey that I would not have been able to complete without the help and encouragement of many wonderful people along the way. Melanie Falick saw promise in this book early on, and shepherded it through thick and thin to make it something I am inordinately proud of. I am grateful to be able to call her both my editor and a friend. Sue McCain's sure hand, eagle eye, and crackerjack sense of humor made her the best tech editor a girl could ask for. Sarah Von Dreele put my vision to paper with her beautiful book design, and photographer Thayer Allyson Gowdy, stylist Viktoria Ruchkan, and their amazing team brought the items in this book to life with their lush, gorgeous images. Moreover, the babies, of course, could not have been sweeter. I'm grateful to them and also to their parents for allowing them to appear in this book.

Vintage Baby Knits would have been impossible without my team of knitters. Laura Prescott tech-edited the patterns in their early stages, knitted the Jackie Sweater, the Betty Lou Lace Cardigan, and the Bobby Kimono, and was generally instrumental in the book's development. Crocheter extraordinaire Lisa Barcy provided her hook, her vintage fabric collection, and her unflagging encouragement. Aushra Abouzeid, who taught me how to knit on a cold Christmas night in Lithuania some 15 years ago, lent me her needles for the Maude Honeycomb Blanket. Alison Aske tirelessly worked on Rupert the Lion, the Oscar Argyle and the Harry Sailor Sweater. Susann Berger knit the Avery Christening Gown and Frock with astonishing speed and grace. Tania Chau did a great job knitting the Billie Beret and some darling Frankie Socks. Grumperina deftly knit the Daisy Soakers, the Frances Nursing Shawl, and the Stella Pixie Hat without blinking an eye. Julia Gibbs was a great help by knitting the Milo Soakers and Horace the Horse. Rae Calado knitted the Floyd Pullover in a flash. Kirsten Johnson brought Elmer the Elephant to life. Margarita Haury's lovely colorwork can be seen in the Gladys Fair Isle Bonnet. Joan Kass spent weeks knitting Frankie Socks and also knit up the gorgeous Hazel Cape. Corey LaFlamme did beautiful work with the Archie Vest and Otto Short-Sleeved Pullover. Linda McCleland, in addition to lending her ear countless times, lent me her needles for the Violet Sacque.

Veronica Ory did a wonderful job knitting and editing the Felix Set and the Jackie Blanket, and Lisa Whiting knitted the Ducky Onesie and Monty pants in the nick of time. I am grateful to have been able to count on all of these knitters for their nimble fingers as well as their wise feedback.

There is not room enough in this book to thank the many people who gave me advice and encouragement as I worked. Cat Bordhi convinced me that I had something worth doing, when I wasn't so sure myself. I depended on both Susan Strawn's wonderful book *Knitting America* and her gracious advice to help shape *Vintage Baby Knits*. Amy Sargent, Mary Beth Temple, and Carol Sulcoski gave me sage advice as well. Elizabeth Morrison lent me her considerable Fair Isle expertise. And Theresa Vinson Stenersen, Sarah Morgan, Tamara Espinal, Maryann Cinelli, Valerie Diden Moore, and the rest of the Chat Girls answered countless impromptu polls and provided endless advice, knitting and otherwise, for two years solid. Vicki Sayre and her wonderful store Loopy Yarns in Chicago took me under their wing when I could barely knit, and helped me come into my own. Amy Cook provided wise counsel, and Lawyers for the Creative Arts helped me navigate unfamiliar territory.

I was able to dedicate myself to this book only because of the love, support, encouragement, and tireless enthusiasm provided by David Hays, my husband, partner, advisor, chief yarn untangler, and friend. He was the first person to see the potential in my idea for *Vintage Baby Knits*, and I have been fortunate enough to be able to depend on him every step of the way. My tolerant friends allowed me to knit through every movie night for the last two years, and my mother and sisters endured more knitting talk than anyone should. I am grateful for their love and their many kindnesses, and for the memory of my wonderful father.

Last but not least, I would like to thank the designers who originated these wonderful patterns. Although we may never know their names, I am very grateful to them for creating designs so very worth revisiting.

About the Author

Kristen Rengren is a Chicago-based knitwear designer whose passion for vintage clothing spans over twenty years. A former vintage clothing dealer, she currently designs for yarn companies and for her own company Retroknit Design (www.retroknit.net).